WOMAN
AGAINST SLAVERY

The Story of Harriet Beecher Stowe

WOMEN OF AMERICA Milton Meltzer, EDITOR

WOMAN AGAINST SLAVERY

The Story of Harriet Beecher Stowe

by John Anthony Scott

Illustrated with Photographs

THOMAS Y. CROWELL COMPANY
NEW YORK

Library of Congress Cataloging in Publication Data

Scott, John Anthony
Woman Against Slavery
(Women of America) Bibliography: p. Includes index.
1. Stowe, Harriet Elizabeth Beecher, 1811–1896—
Biography.   2. Authors, American—19th century—
Biography.   I. Title.
PS2956.S36   818′.3′09 [B]   77-5310
ISBN 0-690-00701-9   0-690-03844-5 (LB)

10   9   8   7   6   5   4   3

For Martha

Acknowledgments

David Parker and the late Caroline Emerson made available to me rare materials in their possession. David Comins, Paul Freedman, Peter Kinoy, Rita Murphy, Joyce Pohs, and Robin Scott helped with research. Mrs. Elizabeth Urbanowicz prepared drafts with accuracy and speed. Arthur Kinoy of the Rutgers University School of Law contributed a searching analysis of A Key to Uncle Tom's Cabin. A number of institutions made available their manuscript collections, notably the Stowe-Day Foundation, the New York Public Library, Columbia University, the Library of Congress, Smith College, the Houghton Library of Harvard University, the Boston Public Library, Radcliffe College, the Massachusetts Historical Society, Yale University, the Henry E. Huntington Library, the Stockbridge Library Association, as did also Lockett F. Ballard, Jr., Director of the Litchfield Historical Society, and Mrs. Barbara Todd, special assistant in the society's library. Many thanks are due to Matilda Welter and Milton Meltzer for the care with which they scrutinized the manuscript and saw it through the press.

Thanks are given to the following for permission to reproduce material: Beecher-Stowe Collection, Schlesinger Library, Radcliffe College; Henry W. and Albert A. Berg Collection, the New York Public Library, Astor Lenox and Tilden Foundations; the Huntington Library, San Marino, California.

CONTENTS

Foreword

Some of the highest praise ever given to Harriet Beecher Stowe as a writer came from a famous black author and poet. Writing in 1952 on the occasion of the one hundredth anniversary of the publication of *Uncle Tom's Cabin,* Langston Hughes called it "the story of a gentle black Christ who turned the other cheek." The book, he said, was "an appeal to the conscience of all men to look upon bondage as a crime." Hughes also praised the "unforgettable children" whom Harriet had created in her novel, and he dwelt feelingly on "the love, and warmth, and humanity that went into its writing and kept it alive."

Harriet Beecher Stowe was indeed a towering figure in nineteenth-century American history. She helped millions of her fellow citizens to become aware of the shame of slavery and to take their place, side by side with black people, in the struggle to end it. She brought to the work of teaching and propaganda a powerful intellect, a compassionate imagination, and a literary talent far beyond the ordinary.

Langston Hughes' awareness of Harriet's stature was, at the time he wrote, a little unusual. In the one hundred years and more that have passed since 1852, "Uncle Tom" has become a household word in the United States; but Harriet Beecher Stowe's contribution as an American writer and thinker has on the whole been forgotten, and her image as a human being has been blurred beyond recognition. From that day to this people have gotten their ideas about her and the *Cabin* not so much from her own writings or from the facts of her own life as from something she detested and wanted no part of—the Tom shows.

Stage versions of *Uncle Tom's Cabin* began to appear in 1852, the very same year that the book was published. These Tom shows, as they were called, became a powerful influence in American public life between the end of the Civil War in 1865 and the outbreak of World War I in 1914. During those years traveling players took the Tom shows to uncounted millions of people both in Europe and America.

The Tom shows were circus-type entertainments featuring blackface minstrels, tap dancing, and buffoonery intermingled with stock episodes from Harriet's book— Eliza, the slave, fleeing across the frozen Ohio River, babe

in arms; Little Eva dying in a big bed surrounded by sob-
bing black people; Simon Legree, the slaveowner, twirling
his mustachios and cracking his whip at Uncle Tom; and
so on.

For nearly three quarters of a century the Tom show was
bread-and-butter for an army of actors. Pure melodrama, it
implanted in the public mind a picture of *Uncle Tom's
Cabin* that had little or no relationship to Harriet's work or
to her original message. It robbed Harriet's black people of
their dignity as suffering, struggling human beings and
turned them into shuffling, grinning figures of fun or
banjo-strumming clowns. Black people played the central
role in Harriet's novel, but in the Tom shows the whites
stole the show. To add insult to injury, the black parts
were played by blacked-up white actors.

Today in the United States for the first time since the
1850s millions of people are trying once again to understand the reality of American slavery and the meaning of
the black experience that has been so deeply intertwined
with it. They are seeking to brush aside the illusions and
the myths that have so long and so effectively veiled this
most tragic aspect of the American past. It is time, therefore, to say good-bye to the Tom shows and the tradition
of lies and racism that they have upheld, and to ask the
real Harriet Beecher Stowe to stand up. It is time to re-
cover the message that she communicated to her own generation and which once again has a profound meaning for
ours. That is what this book is about.

John Anthony Scott

CHAPTER ONE

WHERE THE LONG NIGHT RAIN BEGINS
Childhood, 1811–23

Then up from the glooming meadows
  Through the long night rain and wind
And up from the glooming rainpath,
  Where the long night rain begins
Come the poor lost sheep of the sheepfold
  They all come a-gathering in.

  —*New England Song*

There was once a slaveholder who lived in South Carolina. One day a neighbor came to visit him. The conversation turned to the topic of religion among the slaves.

"Religion among slaves," said the visitor, "is stuff and nonsense. The rascals just *pretend* to believe in God, but they don't really. It's sheer hypocrisy."

"Not so," replied his host, "as a matter of fact I have right here on this plantation a slave who would rather die than deny his Saviour."

"I don't believe a word of it!" said the other. "And I'll bet you can't prove it."

So the owner sent for his religious slave.

"Now, Tom," said he, "tell me right now 'I don't believe in Jesus Christ my Saviour.' That's an order!"

"Excuse me, master," said the slave, "I cannot say those words. I cannot deny my Lord, Jesus Christ, who shed his blood for me."

"By God," swore his master, "say what I told you, or I'll have you whipped till the skin is off your back."

The slave hung his head and remained silent. So his master sent for one of his drivers and had him whipped. As the blows fell he yelled at his victim, "Just say what I told you to, and I'll turn you loose."

But the slave never spoke a word. He received two hundred or more blows from the rawhide and then died.

This story of a slave who chose death rather than submit to the will of his master was first told to the world by Sarah Grimké, herself the daughter of a South Carolina slaveholder and later a leader in the antislavery movement. The tale was published in 1839 in a book called *American Slavery As It Is* in which Theodore Weld, a famous antislavery leader, brought together under a single cover the testimony of many people, black and white, who had witnessed the cruelty of American slavery. When Harriet Beecher Stowe got a copy of this book and read Sarah Grimké's story, some time between 1840 and 1843, she was a young married woman with four small children, very busy running her home in the suburbs of Cincinnati.

American Slavery As It Is became the companion of Harriet's life, and she committed large parts of it to memory. As she herself put it in later years, she "kept the book in her work basket by day, and slept with it under her pillow by night." Many of the horrible things which the book told about haunted her imagination and robbed her of her sleep. She saw the faces of black people in torment, and she heard their screams.

The slave whipped to death because he would not deny Jesus haunted her especially. One Sunday in 1851, after the Stowe family had moved to Brunswick, Maine, Harriet became lost in daydreams during church service and forgot where she was. The picture of the slave being flogged to death came before her eyes, as she put it, "almost as a tangible vision." She went home and at once wrote down what she had seen. It was the death of Uncle Tom and the climax of *Uncle Tom's Cabin,* the novel that, just one year later, would stun the whole world and win a circulation among the peoples of the globe only second to that of the Bible itself.

Harriet Beecher, sixth child of Roxana and Lyman Beecher, the woman who wrote this book, was born in 1811 in Litchfield, a little town that sits upon a hill amid the lovely wooded hills of western Connecticut. She grew to young womanhood in her father's big wooden house on North Street. It was a broad, elm-shadowed road where the minister, the doctor, the lawyer, the sheriff, and the schoolteacher lived in cool, roomy homes set well back from the street and flanked by stately well-tended gardens. The farmers of the township lived out in the countryside all around Litchfield hill. Their houses, as Harriet recalled, "sat on high hills or sunk in deep valleys, and their flam-

ing windows at morning and evening looked through the
encircling belts of forest solitude as if to say 'we are here,
and we are a power.' "

Harriet's first childhood memories were of her mother,
Roxana. She carried through life the image of a beautiful
dark-haired woman in a brown dress who sat in the yard,
while the children played, and chopped mint in a wooden
bowl with a moon-shaped knife. She remembered, too,
many little touches around the house that told of Roxana's
presence: clothes chests hand-painted with little bouquets
of gaily colored flowers set among flowing green tendrils
and intricate patterns of leaves; fine embroidery with a
cobweb stitch, pictures of birds done in minute detail.

In 1815 Roxana received a gift of Dutch tulips from her
brother John. She put the little brown bulbs away in a
closet against the day that she would set them out in the
flower beds around the house. But four-year-old Harriet,
who was always rummaging around, soon found the "on-
ions" and ate them up with the help of her brother
George.

When spring came there were no red and yellow tulips,
and Roxana was very sick. People who met Harriet in the
street asked her how her mother did. When she peeped
into the kitchen closet it was filled with delicacies which
the neighbors were sending in. Once a day Harriet was
allowed to visit the sickroom where Roxana lay propped up
in bed. She remembered "a very fair face, with a bright red
spot on each cheek, and a quiet smile as she offered me a
spoonful of her gruel."

At the end of that summer, in September 1816, Roxana
died. The family, dressed in black, walked to the burial

ground that lay at the foot of the hill below the meeting-house. There was talk at the graveside, and the sound of earth being thrown, and little ones asking, "Where has mama gone?"

"To Heaven," said one adult. "Into the ground," said another. Candace, the black woman who came in each week to do the family washing, didn't say anything. She took Harriet into her arms, and kissed her hands, and wept.

Harriet had two older sisters, Catharine and Mary, and five brothers: William, Edward, and George, who were older than she, and Henry Ward and Charles, who were younger. Many times she went along with the boys on their rambles in the woods. Sometimes they all went fishing. In the fall, armed with every basket that they could find, they went out to gather chestnuts and walnuts. In the fall, too, the winter's wood supply had to be brought in, cut, split, piled, and taken to the woodhouse. This was hard work and it went on for two whole days. The whole family pitched in: Harriet, in the little black coat that made her look like a boy, worked as hard as anybody.

When winter came the snow lay thick on the Connecti-cut hills and the winds howled mournfully in the chimneys. Then the long evenings would be filled with story-telling and music. Father played psalms or Scottish fiddle tunes on his old violin, Catharine or Mary accompanied him on the piano, William and Edward played the flute. These domestic concerts made the whole house ring with melody and song. Harriet would remember the hours thus spent as "among the most cheerful of my life."

Sometimes the boys excluded their little sister from

their fishing trips. Harriet was left behind with nothing to do but sew the hem on a sheet or gaze wistfully out the window at the slow procession of clouds across the sky. When evening came the fishermen would finally return. "What joy," she wrote later, "to hear at a distance the tramp of feet, the shouts and laughs of older brothers; and what glad triumph when the successful party burst into the kitchen with long strings of perch, roach, pickerel and bullheads, with waving blades of wet flag, and high heads of cattail, and pockets full of young wintergreen."

One year after Roxana's death Lyman Beecher remarried. His second wife, named Harriet Porter, was from Portland, Maine; Harriet described her new stepmother as "a beautiful lady, very fair, with bright blue eyes and soft auburn hair." Harriet Porter never succeeded in coming very close to any of Roxana's children, and she never filled the great empty space in their lives that Roxana's death had left. That death was a catastrophe that bound Harriet and her brothers even more closely to their father. His influence in their lives would be a central one.

Lyman Beecher was born in 1775, when the revolutionary war with Britain had already begun and the big guns of the British fleet were bombarding New England's coastal towns. The son of a New Haven farmer and blacksmith, he had been raised in the tradition of rural New England, following the hard life of the self-sufficient farm family that sheared its own sheep, spun and wove its own cloth, raised its own fodder and wheat crops, and hunted for deer, squirrel, and quail in the woods and water meadows.

Lyman Beecher loved life and lived it with an exuberant energy and joy. But he was raised, too, in the traditional New England religion that warned people against the joys and the temptations of life. Old-time New England religion possessed a vivid sense of the shortness of human existence. It urged people to accept the reality of early death and to be prepared, always, for eternity.

The Congregationalists, as these New England Protestants were called, held a view of the universe which, by and large, they had inherited from medieval Europe. God ruled this universe, they thought, both as lawgiver and as judge. They believed that God was angry with men and women because they were always breaking the divine law and so getting into mischief. After the end of the world, they believed, there would be a day of judgment; God would judge everybody for his or her sins. Many people would be sent to the prison of the universe which Christians labeled "hell." In that place wicked people would suffer the torments reserved for those who had willfully broken or defied the law of God.

For sensible people, the Congregationalists thought, there was another option. You might, if you wished, throw yourself upon the mercy of the court. That is, you might plead guilty, confess that you were a sinner and had indeed done wrong, and ask God to forgive you.

Would God really forgive people who had done wrong? The Congregationalists, to tell the truth, were not too sure what the answer was to this one. Most of them would have agreed that there was a good chance that some people, at least, would be saved from hell if they were truly sorry.

They thought that God's anger at man had been a little softened by the pleadings of his son, Jesus. Jesus was like a lawyer for the defense. He was always urging his father, God, to grant men and women a full pardon if they were indeed truly sorry for what they had done.

But the point was this. If you were going to avoid eternal damnation and be "saved" from hell, you had to start right now (this very moment) feeling sorry for your sins. You had to commit your soul to Jesus' care, and pray to him to help you make it.

The awful meaning of eternal punishment dawned upon Lyman Beecher when he was a child of ten. It was Sunday evening and the boy was out playing in the fields. In those days the rule was that both work and play on Sundays were sinful, because Sunday was God's day and must be devoted to prayer. The holy day was over, according to this rule, as soon as night drew on and three stars were clearly visible in the sky.

But Lyman was eager to play, and he didn't wait for any three stars. Another boy saw him and called out, "That's wicked; there ain't three stars."

"Don't care," Lyman replied.

"God says you mustn't," said the other boy.

"Don't care," said Lyman.

"He'll punish you!"

"Well, if he does, I'll tell Aunt Benton."

"Well, he's bigger than Aunt Benton, and he'll put you in the fire and burn you for ever and ever."

Lyman knew what fire was, and what "forever" meant. That night he cried himself to sleep thinking about a life of suffering that would go on forever, without end.

When Lyman Beecher grew older, the saving of people's souls became to him a matter of terrible urgency. In eighteenth-century New England there were many ways to die, and many people did indeed die young. There were "wasting fevers" like the one that took Roxana's life, there were rattlesnakes lurking in forest and meadow, there were falling trees, kicking horses, thunderbolts, and rivers in flood. People, so Beecher thought, must repent their sins and be prepared to die at any moment. For who knew, when he left home in the morning, if he would come back at night?

Lyman Beecher was ordained as a Congregationalist minister in 1799. From his first pastorate in Easthampton on Long Island he launched in the following year a revivalist movement almost without equal in the history of American religion. Ministers like Beecher were called revivalists because they sought to revive, or reawaken, the sense of sin and the fear of God in the minds of heedless and unrepentant people.

To accomplish his goal, Beecher traveled incessantly— by boat, by coach, or on horseback. He gave sermons in the meetinghouses of the communities that he visited, and some of these were ordination sermons—that is to say, talks delivered at ceremonies when new ministers were formally admitted to their pastoral duties. He spoke at church assemblies of various types; and he addressed special groups which the church had helped set up, like Bible Societies, Temperance Unions, and Missionary groups. Many of these sermons were published as tracts, or pamphlets, and were read by people throughout the country. Thus when Beecher moved with his wife and growing fam-

ily to Litchfield in 1810 he already had a reputation that
was nationwide.

All this traveling meant that Beecher was often away
from home, so that Roxana had to bear more than her
share of the household burdens. On one occasion she complained to Lyman about his frequent absences, but he lectured her on "the duty of resignation." On another occasion—it was January 1811 and Roxana was three
months pregnant with Harriet—she complained to her
sister-in-law Esther that "Mr. Beecher is gone to preach at
New Hartford, and did not provide us wood enough to
last, seeing the weather has grown so bitterly cold."

Beecher's neglect of family duties may have worked a
hardship upon Roxana, and even contributed to her early
death. But it would be difficult to reproach Lyman with
neglecting his children. He loved his family, delighted in
their companionship, and after Roxana's death assumed
full responsibility for their spiritual welfare. When they
went fishing, Lyman went with them; when they worked
at their household chores, like getting in the winter wood
supply, Lyman was there. And, during the winter evenings he talked with them endlessly about the meaning of
the world and about the destiny of truly Christian people.
To all his children he was not only father and friend, but
also teacher.

Lyman had great hopes that all of his and Roxana's boys
would follow in his footsteps and become preachers; and,
as a matter of fact, they all did. As for Harriet, he studied
his daughter closely. In 1819, at the age of eight, she was
a tiny girl, not much more than four feet high, with wavy
chestnut hair and dark gray eyes. She was a studious,

thoughtful person and very, very intelligent. Harriet, Lyman told himself, is a genius! What a shame she was a girl—if she had been a boy, she too would have made a fine minister to carry on his revivalist work.

Harriet adored her father. In later years she would recall that "the very touch of his hand seemed to put strength into me and his brisk joyful footstep at the door made me feel as if I had someone coming on whom I could lean all my cares." His sermons with their force and eloquence made a deep impression upon her; and it was from Lyman that she received her first lesson on the inhumanity of slavery. In 1820 the question was before Congress, Whether Missouri should be admitted to the Union as a free or slave state? Beecher on this occasion passionately opposed the spread of slavery to new lands across the Mississippi. She would never forget the sermons of that time in which he told about the evil of slavery and the sufferings of the slave. His preaching, she remembered later, "drew tears from the hardest faces of the old farmers of his congregation." Her father's words and prayers "indelibly impressed my heart and made me what I am from my very soul, the enemy of all slavery."

Harriet had a passion for physical activity, like working on the woodpile, or exploring the hills and forests around Litchfield and the Bantam River that splashed and gurgled its way through the pine groves to the east of the Beecher home. But she was also a dreamer; any time of the day, or even in the middle of a conversation, there was no telling when her mind would wander off, and she would be utterly lost in a world of her own making.

Harriet delighted to dream about her beloved New England. She would seat herself on the rough granite steps outside the front door of the house with some favorite book. After a while the book would fall from her hand, and she would be far away in the cool forest depths amid the beauties of the wilderness, amid, as she recalled later, "the crisp apples of the pink azalea, the scarlet wintergreen berries, the pink shell blossoms of trailing arbutus, the blue and white, and yellow violets, and crowfoot, and bloodroot, and wild anemone." Standing in that same doorway she would feast her eyes on the panorama of the hills, Mount Tom rearing its blue head to the sky, and the distant glint of Bantam Pond. Or she would sit for hours at the parlor window "watching the glory of the wonderful sunsets that used to burn themselves out, amid voluminous wreathings or castellated turrets of clouds."

Harriet was not only a dreamer but also a bookworm. By the time she was six years old she had learned to read and had developed a passion for reading. She ransacked the house from cellar to attic in search of reading material to feed her imagination and to satisfy her curiosity about the world.

There was very little in Lyman's theological library to fire the enthusiasm of this young romantic. Lyman's shelves were packed with dry-as-dust stuff. They were a barren waste of sermons, treatises, and tracts. Harriet searched patiently, hour after hour, amid this mass of material—in closets, on the shelves, in barrels in the attics—in the hope of finding something worth reading.

Once in a while her efforts were rewarded by a real gem. On one occasion she discovered a tattered copy of Cervantes' *Don Quixote,* which had come apart at the seams and was lying around in several pieces. On another occasion she unearthed a copy of the *Arabian Nights.* This opened up for Harriet a world even more enchanting than the forest that lay all around her. As she read, Harriet soon forgot where she was and lost track of time. She walked among genii and fairies, amid jeweled trees and enchanted palaces. She made friends with Sinbad the Sailor and polished the magic lamps in Aladdin's palace.

The novels of Sir Walter Scott were one of Harriet's greatest discoveries during the Litchfield years. Novels, as she so well knew, were not to be found in the homes of serious-minded ministers like her father. Such people thought that novels showed human wickedness in an attractive light; and such books were the work of the devil. But, quite by accident, Sir Walter Scott's literary works came into the Beecher household in 1822. Lyman went over these books; after much reflection he decided that his children might read them. "I have always disapproved of novels as trash," he said, "but in these there is real genius and real culture, and you may read them."

What a summer that was for Harriet! She read *Ivanhoe* not once, but many times. She committed parts of it to memory. Soon, she tells us, she was able "to recite many of its scenes, from beginning to end, word for word." From Sir Walter Scott she learned the art of storytelling.

Another of Harriet's precious finds at this time was the poetry of George Gordon Byron, the English poet who, when she was a child, was taking the English-speaking world by storm. The passion and the power of Byron's writing enchanted her, and when he died in 1824 Harriet felt that she had lost one of her closest friends. "I was too dispirited to do anything," she recalled later, "so I lay down among the daisies, and looked up into the blue sky, and thought of the great eternity into which Byron had entered, and wondered how it might be with his soul."

In the autumn of 1822, when the apple harvest was in, applesauce had to be made and stored in barrels in the cellar—in those days country families used applesauce on their bread instead of butter. Lyman sat in the kitchen working the apple-peeler. "Come, George," he said, "I'll tell you what we'll do to make the evening go off. You and I'll take turns and see who'll tell the most out of Scott's novels." So the whole evening long George and Lyman peeled apples and turned Scott's novels into yarns, while Harriet listened quiet and open-eyed.

Even when Harriet was a tiny child she impressed her family with her memory. By the time she was four she had learned dozens of hymns by heart and whole chapters from the Bible. She was a very observant person, and nothing escaped her attention. She remembered everything—not only what people did and said, but also their very looks. When she was a middle-aged woman she was able to recall the faces of people so vividly that she could draw pictures of them even though she had not seen those people for forty years or more.

When Harriet was growing up in Litchfield there were black people in the community as well as white. Litchfield, by 1800, was a prosperous place where wealthy merchants lived in fine houses. The town served the needs of

the farmers and pioneers who had settled amid the surrounding hills, and it was an important communication
center on the roads that led from New Haven and Boston
to the Hudson Valley. In the eighteenth century Litchfield
people had owned slaves and thought nothing of it; but by
1800, they were setting them free.

Julius Deming, for example, a wealthy Litchfield mer-
chant and landowner, emancipated his slave girl Vira in
1801, and the deed was filed in the town records. "Vira,"
he testified, "having been born a slave by the laws of this
State, and having arrived at the age of twenty-five years, is
now desirous to be made free. . . . Now know ye that the
said Servant Girl Vira is . . . fully emancipated and made
free."

In the olden days slavery had indeed been lawful in all
the New England colonies. From the seventeenth century
until well after the Revolution many thousand black slaves
toiled in New England as craftsmen, dock workers, farm-
hands, sailors, and house servants. But Thomas Jefferson's
Declaration of Independence and the Revolution that followed it brought about a change for the New England
slaves. They fought in the militia forces and in the Conti-
nental armies, and they were promised their freedom in return.

In the years that followed the end of the revolutionary
war slavery in Connecticut, as elsewhere in New England,
was a dying institution. The American Constitution outlawed the importation of slaves into the United States after
1808. While the Southern states permitted black people to
be held as slaves, and to be bought and sold even after that

date, New England followed a different path. A law passed by the Connecticut legislature in 1784 made provision that all children born into slavery in the state after that year would become free at the age of twenty-five. When Harriet was born there were still some ten thousand people being held as slaves in New England. But in ten more years this number would dwindle to almost nothing.

CHAPTER TWO

FOR THOSE IN PERIL
School, 1819–29

O hear us when we cry to thee
For those in peril on the sea.

—Mariners' Hymn

In 1819, at the age of eight, Harriet began to attend Miss Sally Pierce's Litchfield Female Academy. There, along with about eighty other girls, she was given the genteel education that was considered proper for women in those days. She embroidered decorative pieces which showed funeral scenes—a tombstone, a willow tree, weeping mourners whose faces were almost entirely hidden by their flowing pocket handkerchiefs. And she embroidered pastoral scenes—fair young shepherdesses sitting on green grassy banks with crooks in their hands, while woolly lambs grazed all around.

Needlework, drawing, and music were the skills that most of the old-fashioned New England female academies took it for granted were the most useful preparation for a woman's life. But Sally Pierce's school was unusual because it also taught science, languages, and the classics. Harriet's teacher for these subjects was Miss Pierce's nephew, John Pierce Brace; he was an important influence in her life and, by all accounts, one of the most dynamic schoolteachers of his time.

John Pierce Brace lived in a cottage two doors down the road from the Beechers. Brace took his students out into the fields and woods on long tramps to collect the different kinds of rocks that were to be found in the Litchfield neighborhood. "There was," Harriet recalled, "scarcely a ledge of rocks within a circuit of twelve miles that had not resounded to the tap of his stone hammer, and furnished specimens for his collection."

Brace opened up wonderful new worlds for the students who thronged around him on these walks and who listened to him with fascination in the classroom. Botany, geology, history, and literature were subjects upon which he delighted to discourse. "Brace," Harriet said, "held us all by the sheer force of his personality, character and will, just as the ancient mariner held the wedding guest with his glittering eye." The man put his students' minds into a ferment; he drove them on, by a very personal inspiration, to think, to work, and to write. "He so utterly scorned and despised a lazy scholar," wrote Harriet, "that trifling and inefficiency in study were scorched and withered by the very breath of his nostrils. . . . His praise bore a value in proportion to its scarcity."

John Pierce Brace, among his many other accomplishments, taught rhetoric and composition—the art, that is, of setting down ideas clearly and systematically on paper and communicating them simply and forcefully through the spoken word. He divided the girls into groups to write compositions in turn. When, in addition, he asked for volunteers for this kind of work, Harriet was one student who never failed to respond. In these papers the students explored the merits of Milton and Shakespeare, criticized the newspaper editorials that Brace supplied them with, and wrote sarcastic attacks upon some pompous and windy Fourth of July oration.

John Pierce Brace, too, encouraged his students to debate issues by exploring one or the other side of a question that he presented for their consideration. One such question that he came up with in the fall of 1822 was the following: Can the immortality of the soul be proven by "the light of nature"?

Harriet, then only a child of eleven, took up this theme and composed an essay. Common sense, she wrote, tells us that people live for a little while and then they pass away forever; they vanish from the earth without leaving a trace, and the world goes on as though they had never been. Human beings are like flowers; they come into bloom, they bloom for a tiny span of time, and then they slowly fade away. At the very end of man's life we see only the sad ruin of the lovely youth that once was. Soon the tomb will hold all that remains of a human being, a handful of silent dust.

Such, concluded Harriet, is the meaning of life if we read it by the light of nature and experience. But how hard it is for us to accept this fact! We want so much to live forever! Is there any possible proof, Harriet asked herself, contrary to the blunt and cruel evidence of nature, that the human soul *does* survive the changes of time and the physical death that overtakes all living things?

Here Harriet drew an answer from the promises of the Bible that she had so carefully read and from the long winter evening conversations with her father. Christ's coming to earth, she told her readers, was an event that changed the thinking of mankind. It provided a promise, and a certainty, that there would be a life to come.

Harriet shaped her thoughts and composed her essay with the help of John Pierce Brace. It was a very good piece of writing, beautifully and feelingly written; and it testified both to the skill of the teacher and the natural literary talent of the pupil. In this writing Harriet expressed with style, conviction, and clarity her belief that the Gospel, as a statement of God's will and law, plays a central part in human experience.

John Brace found Harriet's essay so good that he read it out loud at the annual reading of the outstanding student compositions in 1823; and it stirred much comment. "I remember the scene at the exhibition," Mrs. Stowe wrote many years later: "The hall was crowded with the literati of Litchfield. Before them all our compositions were read aloud. When mine was read, I noticed that father, who was sitting on high by Mr. Brace, brightened and looked interested, and at the close I heard him say, 'Who wrote that composition?' '*Your daughter, sir!*' was the answer. It was the proudest moment of my life."

Harriet's essay was an expression of her faith in immortality and in the Christian revelation—a faith that never left her as long as she lived. It was also her response to a tragedy that had just occurred in the Beecher family. In mid-June 1822, when the Litchfield laurel was coming into bloom, news arrived that the packet ship *Albion,* which had sailed from New York City in April, had been lost at sea. The ship had gone down with all hands off the coast of Ireland. Among those lost was Alexander Fisher, a brilliant young professor of mathematics at Yale, who was engaged to be married to Catharine Beecher.

Catharine, Lyman and Roxana's firstborn child, was twenty-two years old when she received this news. Born at Easthampton in 1800, she adored her father and modeled herself in his image. She and Lyman rode horseback together or took long tramps over the sands along the Long Island seashore. Catharine, like her father, loved to mix with people and to travel. Never in her life could she be bounded by the four walls of a home and find it enough. Harriet admired her sister, who was eleven years older than she, and also stood a little in awe of her. She described Catharine as somebody who was so very intellectual that she didn't really seem to be a creature of flesh and blood at all; and she was certainly not a woman to accept without protest the conventional position then assigned to women in American society. "She never could have made," as Harriet wrote later, "one of those clinging, submissive, parasitical wives who form the delight of song and story, and are supposed to be the peculiar gems of womanhood."

When Roxana died in 1816 Catharine took her mother's

place for a while; she went to work sewing, cooking, and keeping house. When Lyman married Harriet Porter in 1817 Catharine gave over her household duties with relief, and her role as a homemaker came to an end. In 1821, after spending several joyful and carefree years in Litchfield, she left her father's home and went to earn her living as a teacher in a New London girls' school. That year, too, she met Alexander Fisher. The couple became engaged in 1822 just before Fisher left for Europe on the packet ship *Albion*.

When the news of Fisher's death arrived, Lyman Beecher could do little to comfort Catharine. The waves of the Atlantic, he told her, had snatched her lover away from her. It was God's will. Had Fisher gone to Heaven or to Hell? There was no way, said Lyman, of knowing for sure. Lyman advised his daughter to accept the situation calmly and to submit her will in all things to the will of God.

Catharine, as we might expect, was in no mood to accept this kind of consolation. By what right, she asked herself, did God compel woman to bring forth life, only to see that life handed over to eternal torment? She gazed at her little half sister Isabella, then a babe of four months, as she lay in her cradle; and terrible thoughts passed through Catharine's mind. "When I look at little Isabella," she wrote to her brother Edward, "it seems a pity that she was ever born, and that it would be a mercy if she was taken away."

Thus Catharine's days in the summer of 1822 were filled with despair. She brooded on the horrors of the dark night and the howling storm, and she tried to imagine her lover's agony as he faced death alone and unprepared.

Harriet too had to face Catharine's loss, and she had to find a way of sharing this loss with her older sister. The essay that she wrote under John Brace's guidance was her own way of exploring and coming to terms with a family tragedy that touched her quietly, privately, but deeply. Alexander Fisher's death came six years after the death of Roxana. Both losses taught Harriet that when you love deeply you may also suffer deeply, because you have a chance to lose the person you love. Hope and faith in the goodness of God and the immortality of the human soul offered the only consolation and protection from life's ever-present risk of tragedy and loss.

Apart from all of this, Fisher's death was to have an immediate impact upon Harriet's life. Fisher in his will left Catharine not merely his library—which included the volumes of Sir Walter Scott, which Harriet would read from cover to cover in the summer of 1822—but a bequest of $2,000, a sum which, in terms of modern money, would have been worth $20,000 at the very least. Catharine decided to use this money to launch a girls' school in Hartford. Discussions with the Reverend Joel Hawes, a Hartford minister and one of her father's friends, convinced her that there was a great need for such a school and that the well-to-do people in Hawes' congregation would send their children to it.

So Catharine made her preparations and opened the Hartford Female Academy in May 1823 with fifteen students. She first rented a room above a harness shop on

Main Street; then, as the school expanded, she moved it into the basement of the North Meeting House. Soon the school was a resounding success, and by 1826 the number of pupils had risen to 180. Catharine then built a brand-new schoolhouse, and by 1827 was operating with a full-time staff of eight teachers. The Female Academy won fame as a pioneer experiment in women's education, and made Catharine's reputation as a leading New England educator. Her school continued the tradition that John Pierce Brace had established at Litchfield—it taught young women serious subjects like history, science, classical literature, and modern languages in addition to the more "genteel" subjects of painting, singing, and needlework.

In 1824 Catharine insisted that Harriet should leave Litchfield and come to school in Hartford. Lyman Beecher was not unhappy to see his daughter join the Hartford Female Academy. What could be better for Harriet, he asked himself, than to be a student in a first-rate girls' school under Catharine's supervision? And so it was decided. In the fall of 1824 Harriet packed her bag and took the coach to Hartford. She was to board in the home of Mrs. Isaac Bull, wife of a Hartford druggist. Mrs. Bull's daughter, in return, was to live in Litchfield and board at the Beechers.

The Hartford years, which stretched from 1824 till 1832, were a period of deep unhappiness in Harriet's life. Growing up in the Hartford Female Academy under the supervision of sister Catharine was a lonely and painful experience.

Harriet was tormented by homesickness. At the age of

thirteen she had suddenly lost her beloved Litchfield home
and the companionship of her father and brothers. It is
true that she went back to Litchfield for the summer vaca-
tion of 1825; but this proved to be the last summer that
she would ever spend in the little Berkshire town she loved
so well. In the early spring of 1826, when the snow was
still deep on the Connecticut hills, Lyman Beecher himself
left Litchfield and moved to Boston to become the minister
of the Hanover Street Church in Boston's North End.

Lyman Beecher made this decision with regret. He too
loved Litchfield, its lakes, woods, hills, and delightful
walks. It pained him to leave the burial ground where
Roxana lay, the house and yard with its big vegetable garden, the cows grazing quietly in the orchard; the orchard
that produced each year a shower of apples, enough not
only for apple butter but for many barrels of cider.

Lyman was sad about leaving, but in truth he had no
choice. His salary as pastor of the Litchfield Congregational Church was hardly enough to live on, and, in addition, he still had four boys to put through college. In
1826 George, Lyman's third son, was in college, and this
was costing $400 a year when Lyman's entire annual salary
was only $800. And then after George, Henry Ward and
Charles, Harriet's younger brothers, would have to be sent
to college, to say nothing of Thomas, Harriet Porter's son,
who had been born in 1824.

Lyman was determined that no matter what the cost he
would give his boys the education they needed to follow in
his footsteps and become ministers of Christ. For this purpose he had scrimped, gone without new clothes and a car-

riage, fallen into debt, and neglected to repair his fences and paint his house. But it had all proved in vain. There was never enough money to make both ends meet, much less put anything aside for the future. There was nothing for it but to find a job that paid more.

And so Lyman Beecher left Litchfield and moved to a new home on Sheafe Street in Boston. Like Harriet, he was terribly unhappy with the change; unlike her, he soon rallied with enthusiasm to the new work that lay ahead of him. What place, he asked himself, was more ripe than Boston for a revivalist movement? Over the years the Boston people had become fashionable, successful, and affluent. They scoffed at orthodox religion with its talk of hellfire and damnation. To bring such people back to the fear of God—would not this, Lyman asked himself, be a holy work?

As for Harriet Porter, she shared her husband's enthusiasm for his Boston crusade. "This soil," she told her friends, "was pressed by the feet of the Pilgrims, and watered by their tears. Here are their tombs, and here are their children who are to be brought back to the fold of Christ."

If in 1824 Harriet lost her childhood friends and associates, she won in Hartford very few new friends in whose companionship she might find support, and in whom she might confide. Sister Catharine was more of a guardian than a friend. She took her position of older sister and mother-substitute very seriously, and she gave Harriet many lectures about growing up, shouldering her responsibilities, and taking life seriously.

In 1822, for example, just a few months before Alexander Fisher was lost on the *Albion,* Harriet had gone to visit her mother's family, who lived on a farm called Nutplains in Guilford, Connecticut. Catharine at that time wrote her little sister a letter in which she administered the following rather typical lecture. "We all want you home very much," she had written, "but hope you are now where you will learn to stand and sit straight, and hear what people say to you, and sit still in your chair, and learn to sew and knit well, and be a good girl in every particular; and if you don't [now] I am afraid you never will."

Sometimes, of course, Catharine was fun to be with, as when she took Harriet horseback riding; but in any event she was a mature and driving person who was often overbearing and could at times be a bore. Not until years later, after she had written *Uncle Tom's Cabin,* did Harriet find a way to accept Catharine as a friend and an equal rather than as a figure of authority.

While at Catharine's school, Harriet had two friends who were nearer her own age. There was Georgiana May, a student, who became a lifelong friend; and there was Mary Dutton, a New Haven girl who came to teach mathematics in 1828, but stayed only a year. Apart from these two Harriet had no close friends.

Harriet's intense shyness and her studiousness—each was a quality that reinforced the other—isolated her from young people her own age. She put in very long hours studying grammar, French, Italian, and Latin. She spent much time painting and drawing. In addition to this, by 1827, at the age of sixteen, she had become a part-time teacher in the school. Two years later her teaching obligations were full time. We must think of her as a very quiet and shrinking little schoolmarm who must have seemed strange and perhaps slightly frightening to the other students.

Harriet had deep and passionate feelings, which she hid from the world; her inability both to give love to others and to receive it from them tormented her. She did her best to reach out and make friends, but all these efforts ended in failure and rejection. When, at school, she was lonely and withdrawn, Catharine lectured her for absentmindedness and unsociability. When, visiting Boston during the summers, she tried to conceal her sorrows and to appear cheerful and happy, Lyman Beecher lectured her for loud behavior or for laughing too much. And then, when she took refuge in her own dreams and didn't hear what people said to her, everybody forgot about not laughing loudly, and laughed loudly at her.

And so Harriet passed sleepless nights and choked her groans into a pillow that was wet with tears. "I don't know," she confided to Georgiana, "as I am fit for anything, and I have thought that I could wish to die young and let the remembrance of me and my faults perish in the grave rather than live, as I fear I do, a trouble to everyone."

Harriet had one consolation during the long summers in Boston. Edward was there. Edward Beecher was eight years older than she, and, even though she loved all her brothers dearly, in some sense he was her favorite. He graduated from Yale University in 1822 and then became headmaster of the Hartford Grammar School for Boys. But he left Hartford at just about the same time that Harriet arrived there and went on to study for the ministry at the Theological Seminary in Andover, Massachusetts. In 1826 Edward was ready for his first position as a minister, at the Park Street Church in Boston. He was ordained there in February 1827 with his father preaching the sermon. "I believe the field before you is white to the harvest," Lyman told his son, "God send you soon to reap."

Edward at the Park Street Church was a great comfort to Harriet during the years 1827 to 1830. She confided in her brother about the bitter loneliness in which she lived. Edward reproached her for her coldness, for the aloofness she showed toward other members of the family. Harriet tearfully admitted the truth of the reproach; but, she told her brother, her feelings were dammed up inside her. She did indeed have deep feelings of love toward the family and other people, but, as she put it, "the stronger the affection, the less inclination I have to express it." Could a Christian woman, she asked him, truly love God if she were not also involved with her own kind?

These talks with Edward may have done little to solve Harriet's personal problems, but they were nevertheless of great help to her. Edward was warm and sympathetic, and she learned much from his wise advice and his sturdy common sense. "Somehow or other," she told him, "you have such a reasonable way of saying things, that when I come to reflect I almost always go over to your side." Years later, when Edward published a great theological work, *The Conflict of the Ages,* Harriet told her friends that he was speaking for her as well as for himself.

In the summer of 1829 a young man in Lyman Beecher's congregation was about to leave New England and travel south to become the editor of an antislavery paper in Baltimore. A printer by trade, he was at that time twenty-four years of age and his name was William Lloyd Garrison. The Boston Congregational churches invited him to deliver a Fourth of July sermon before his departure; and so it was arranged. Garrison made his speech in Edward Beecher's Park Street Church, and Edward himself sat on the platform beside Garrison. Harriet, happy as ever to be with her brother, was in the audience.

If people on this occasion expected the usual type of July 4th harangue they must have been shocked at what they heard. The words that fell upon their ears were angry; the speaker's eloquence was passionate and disturbing. "The Fourth of July," the young orator told his listeners, "is the worst and most disastrous day in the whole three hundred and sixty-five." This day, he said, no longer proclaims the rights of man and summons the American people to do battle for them; within a half century of the Revolution it has become simply an occasion for drunkenness, fireworks, and pompous talk.

It is time, Garrison went on, to wake up and face reality. Once it was the British who threatened the survival of the American Union. That struggle is over and won; now we face a new threat to our survival—slavery. The peril that slavery presents to all of us, he told the congregation, is so great that it should make July 4th a day, not of merriment and pageantry, but of fasting and prayer. I come before you, he said, "to obtain the liberation of two million wretched beings who are pining in hopeless bondage—over whose sufferings scarcely an eye weeps, or a

heart melts, or a tongue pleads either to God or man."
And, he added, so long as human beings are held as slaves
in this country "our destruction is not only possible, but
certain."

In 1829 there were indeed two million black slaves in
the United States, whereas fifty years earlier, when the
Revolution came to an end, there had been only 750,000.
Garrison was drawing the attention of his audience to a
stark fact: slavery was not dying out in the Republic, but,
on the contrary, was growing every year by leaps and
bounds.

True enough, slavery had been diminishing rapidly in
New England, but at the same time it had been growing
even more rapidly in the South as the production of cotton
spread rapidly throughout the region during the years
1800–30. Cotton was a crop that could be grown cheaply
and on a large scale with slave labor; and it could be
profitably exported to feed the spinning and weaving ma-
chines of factories in New Jersey, Rhode Island, Massachusetts, England, France, and Belgium. Thus, in the
few short years when Harriet was growing up, slavery had
become a growing, thriving institution. More and more
Americans were being born each year not into the free
country for which so many fighters of the Revolution had
fought and died but into a world of slavery.

William Lloyd Garrison felt that the United States
could not survive if this situation was allowed to continue.
And so he rose in Edward Beecher's church to utter a
warning cry, to point out to Americans the rocks ahead, to
urge them to take action before it was too late.

There is, he said, only one question before us at this

time: What, as Christians, ought we to *do* about the existence of slavery in our land?

"The slaves of this country," Garrison said, "are entitled to the prayers, sympathies, and charities of the American people." This answer to the question that he had posed was not quite as simple as it sounded. Until 1830 few Americans had wasted their sympathies on the slaves; the great majority of white people could not have cared less about the slaves and the wrongs that were being inflicted upon them. Garrison was now asking these people to become concerned about slavery as a menace to America, to become concerned about slaves as human beings with inalienable rights. He was calling for a revolution in public opinion that would cause the American people to say: "Enough! We will not allow slavery to exist in this country any longer."

A little more than twenty years later the great change in public opinion of which he dreamed *did* come about; and the eighteen-year-old Harriet then listening to his words played an important part in producing it. We do not know, of course, what her immediate reaction was to Garrison's message. Up to that time, absorbed as she was with the problems and pains of growing up, she had given little thought to the predicament of the American slaves. The time was not far distant, though, when she would be paying very close attention to what Garrison had said.

Harriet as a young woman   *Courtesy New York Public Library Picture Collection*

The Beecher house in Litchfield, Connecticut, as it is today

Courtesy New York Public Library Picture Collection

Lyman Beecher (*above, left*), Henry Ward Beecher (*above, right*), William Lloyd Garrison (*below, left*) *Courtesy New York Public Library Picture Collection* Elijah P. Lovejoy (*below, right*) *Culver Pictures*

The Cincinnati riverfront and Lane Seminary, as they looked in the mid-nineteenth century
Culver Pictures

Harriet and Calvin Stowe   *Courtesy New York Public Library Picture Collection*

Bowdoin College (*above*), title page of the first edition of *Uncle Tom's Cabin* (*left*),
Josiah Henson, whose autobiography was one of the sources for Uncle Tom (*right*)
Courtesy New York Public Library Picture Collection

UNCLE TOM'S CABIN;

OR,

LIFE AMONG THE LOWLY.

BY

HARRIET BEECHER STOWE.

VOL. I.

BOSTON:
JOHN P. JEWETT & COMPANY.
CLEVELAND, OHIO:
JEWETT, PROCTOR & WORTHINGTON.
1852.

FIRST EDITION, IN THE EXCESSIVELY RARE

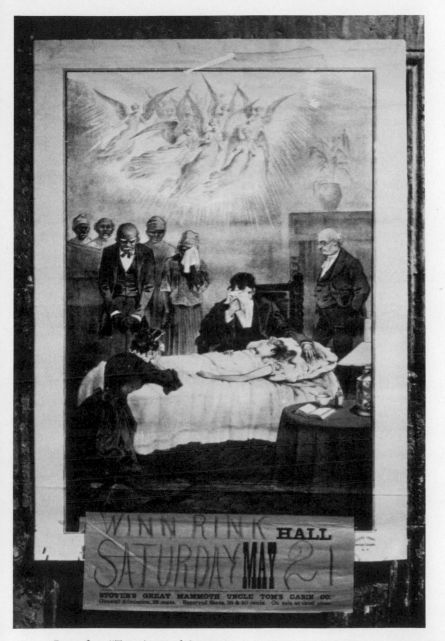

Poster for a "Tom show" of the 1890's

Courtesy New York Public Library Picture Collection

Harriet in 1876   *Culver Pictures*

The Stowe house in Hartford, Connecticut

Courtesy New York Public Library Picture Collection

CHAPTER THREE

TO COME A-GATHERIN' IN
To the West, 1830–34

And he's calling, calling
Calling softly,
For them all to come a-gatherin' in.

—*New England Song*

In May 1832 Harriet was finishing up yet another long year at the Hartford Female Academy, and she was running the school in her sister's absence. Catharine was away with her father, visiting Lane Theological Seminary in Cincinnati, Ohio, where Lyman had been offered the position of college president. She wrote Harriet a letter that described the Cincinnati scene with enthusiasm. "The city," she told Harriet, "does not impress you as being very new. It is true everything looks neat and clean, but it is compact, and a great number of houses are of brick, and very handsomely built. The streets run at right angles to each other, and are quite wide and well paved."

Half the country at that time, or so it seemed, was moving out west. A kind of national mania had set in as eastern people pulled up their stakes and hastened away to the wild, fertile, and beautiful Mississippi Valley.

The churches, too, were sending young men west to organize new congregations on the frontier and to build meetinghouses. They were also setting up western colleges to train ministers to be the spiritual leaders of the region in the years to come. Idealistic young men, who wanted to devote their lives to church and community, were flocking west with everybody else.

Edward Beecher was the first of the Beechers to respond to the western challenge. In 1830, just one year after Garrison had given the July 4th address in the Park Street Church, Edward preached his own farewell sermon there, said good-bye to Harriet and the rest of the family, and set out for Jacksonville, Illinois. He was headed for a post as president of a new school there, Illinois College.

Next it was Lyman's turn. In 1830 Lane Theological Seminary had been founded at Cincinnati by two wealthy New Orleans merchants, Ebenezer and William Lane. The Board of Trustees was composed of an influential group of Cincinnati businessmen and clergy; and they now asked themselves whom they ought to appoint as president of their college. Lane was located at the very gateway to the Midwest. It was sure, they told themselves, to have a great future.

Lyman Beecher was the logical choice. He was the most popular and prominent preacher in the nation. He was a leader who could bring together dedicated young men at Lane and prepare them properly for the Christian work of

building churches and bringing people to Christ in the
new land. He, if anybody, had the vision to lead a great
revival of religion in the Mississippi Valley.

At the end of 1830 the Board of Trustees of Lane Seminary offered Lyman Beecher the job of president. This was
an offer that attracted him very much. Matters had not
been going as well for Lyman in Boston as he had hoped
they would: his message, which had such an appeal for
people in rural America, fell upon deaf ears in New England's sophisticated capital. Edward, Lyman told himself,
was right. The west was the place where a revivalist leader
ought to be—this was the place destined by God and history to be the great American battleground in the struggle
between Christ and the Devil for the soul of America. "To
the west," Lyman concluded, "I will go; and my family
will go with me to support me in my work and to carry on
what I have begun."

So Lyman went to Lane Seminary to look the place over
and to meet the Trustees; and he took Catharine with him.
Catharine was as anxious as her father to make the break,
leave Hartford and move west. By 1830 the Hartford Female Academy was failing. Catharine's ambition had been
to turn out young women who in every sense of the word,
intellectually, emotionally, and morally, were independent
beings. But the Hartford business community, from which
most of her support came, reacted coldly to her ideas. Such
education, these leaders told themselves, was subversive of
the established order: How could women so trained ever
make good, dutiful, and submissive wives?

Catharine's enthusiasm for Cincinnati and Lane Semi-

nary was fired in part by her desire to be free and to start
afresh. "We reached Cincinnati in three days from Wheeling," she told Harriet, "and soon felt ourselves at home.
The next day father and I walked out to Walnut Hills.
The site of the Seminary is very beautiful and picturesque.
It is located on a farm of one hundred and twenty acres of
fine land, with fine groves of trees around it, about two
miles from the city."

Harriet was carried along by her sister's enthusiasm;
there was a place for her too in Catharine's plans. Catharine intended to launch a new school in Cincinnati, and of
course she would need Harriet's help in so important a
venture. Cincinnati, Catharine told her, spelled both economic independence and a happy life. "I know of no place
in the world," she assured Harriet, "where there is so fair a
prospect of finding everything that makes social and domestic life pleasant. . . . The folks here are anxious to
have a school on our plan set on foot here. They have fine
rooms in the city college building, which is now unoc-
cupied, and everybody is ready to lend a hand."

On that visit in April 1832 Lyman Beecher formally accepted the post offered to him. He would have an assured
income not only as president of Lane Seminary but as pastor of the Second Presbyterian Church in Cincinnati. Then
he and Catharine hastened back east to set their affairs in
order and to make preparations for a family migration to
the West. As for Harriet, she packed her trunk and set out
to spend the summer at Nutplains, where she would wait
until the rest of the family was ready to leave. The project
that she took with her to work on was a children's geography which Catharine had suggested that she write.

To Harriet, Nutplains, next to Litchfield, was the most beautiful place in the world. It was a white farmhouse in Guilford, Connecticut, the home where Harriet's mother had been raised, and where her grandmother, Roxana Ward Foote, still lived. Harriet's first visit to her grandmother's home had been directly following Roxana's death, when she was a child of five. Grandmother Foote had bright white hair and wore a great gold ring upon her finger. Harriet loved her dearly.

Harriet delighted, along with her brothers, to explore the rambling old house and to browse through the books in the well-stocked library. She spent hours talking to her uncles and aunts and listening to their tales. "Our hours spent at Nutplains," she recalled later on, talking of these visits with her brothers, "were the golden hours of our life. At Nutplains, our mother, lost to us, seemed to live again. We saw her paintings, her needlework, and heard a thousand little sayings and doings of her daily life." For Harriet, truly, Nutplains was a kind of paradise. "Every juniper bush, every wild sweetbriar, every barren sandy hillside, every stony pasture, spoke of bright hours of love, when we were welcomed back to Nutplains as to our mother's heart."

In the fall of 1832 it was time to say good-bye to New England and to Nutplains. There were nine in the family party that took ship from Boston early in October. There was Lyman Beecher, his sister Esther and his wife Harriet Porter Beecher with her three small children, Isabella, Thomas, and James. In addition to Catharine and Harriet, George Beecher was also with the group. He was headed for a post as minister of the settlement at Chillicothe, Ohio.

As for the rest of the family, Henry Ward and Charles, Harriet's younger brothers, planned to follow as soon as school was over in the spring of 1833. Henry Ward was a student at Amherst College in Massachusetts and Charles was at Yale. Edward, of course, was already in Illinois. Of all the Beecher children, only two would remain in the east: Mary, who was married and living at Hartford, and William, who was a minister in Rhode Island.

The party traveled by boat from Boston to Philadelphia—with a brief stopover in New York—and then took the stagecoach across Pennsylvania to Wheeling, West Virginia. "If today is a specimen of our journey, it will be very pleasant," Harriet wrote at the end of the first day's stage; "obliging driver, good roads, good spirits, good dinner, fine scenery, and now and then some psalms, hymns and spirituals, for with George on board you may be sure of music of some kind."

Four days later the party had crossed the mountains and arrived in Wheeling. Lyman's original plan had been to take the steamboat down the Ohio River from Wheeling all the way to Cincinnati; Harriet had looked forward to a pleasant and lazy river trip through forests flaming with autumn foliage. But a disappointment was in store. News reached the Beechers at Wheeling that there had been an outbreak of the plague in Cincinnati. Lyman, under the circumstances, was in no hurry to move on. The family dawdled for a whole week in Wheeling and then continued the trip by stagecoach, which, of course, took much longer than the river trip would have. The Beechers got to Cincinnati in the middle of November 1832, when cold weather had set in and the epidemic was over. The journey from Boston had taken them a little more than six weeks.

Lane Seminary, surrounded by 120 acres of its own farmlands, was located at Walnut Hills, a pleasant wooded highland on the edge of Cincinnati. The Beechers settled down in a large brick house on the estate. Immense trees of the primeval forest, beech and oak, shadowed the house and provided in the summertime a deep and cooling shade. There was a broad veranda in the back from which, as one of the children remembered, "we used to watch the tossing of the spectral branches during the fierce gales of autumn and winter, and listen to the roaring of the wind through the forest."

In the spring of 1833 Catharine opened the Western Female Institute in downtown Cincinnati with herself and Harriet as associate principals. In order to be close to the school the sisters moved out of Walnut Hills and boarded in the home of Nathaniel Wright, who was president of the Lane Board of Trustees. Harriet began to explore the city and become familiar with it. Here she would live for seventeen years, from 1833 until 1850. Here she would gather the materials for the writing of *Uncle Tom's Cabin*, which was published in 1852, two years after she had left Cincinnati and had returned to New England.

Cincinnati, or "The Queen City," as it was called, was one of several centers whose rise, after 1800, reflected the rapid growth of population and settlement in the trans-Appalachian West. When George Washington retired from the presidency in 1798 Cincinnati was a mere village. Fifteen years later its population had risen to six thousand, or twice the size of Hartford when Harriet went to school there. When Harriet began to teach in the Western Female Institute in 1833, Cincinnati had become a town of twenty-five thousand and ranked among the biggest urban centers in the country.

One important factor in Cincinnati's rise was the coming of the steamboat, which knit the settlers in the Ohio Valley into a single economic community. The city had become an important service and supply center for the entire surrounding countryside—it manufactured household equipment and farm tools, it brewed beer, and it milled flour. One of the main sources of Cincinnati's wealth was meat, and this meant for the most part the butchery and export of hogs. Visitors noticed pigs wandering everywhere in town; it was as hard to escape them as it was to forget the stench that came from the slaughterhouses.

Cincinnati, like other American cities, paid a price for its rapid growth and new-found affluence. The rich lived in brick houses, the poor in miserable shacks and tenements. Disastrous fires broke out frequently and many lives were lost. Even more dangerous was the bad drainage and the filthy condition of the streets. Swamps and marshes along the riverfront were breeding grounds for mosquitoes, the carriers of malaria. Decaying matter piled up in stagnant pools to poison the water supply and to help spread disease. As a result, the death rate from fever and other contagious infections was high. The people suffered horribly from epidemics that raged in the summer and fall. The poor, of course, suffered much more than the rich, many of whom had summer homes in the nearby resort community of Yellow Springs.

Cholera was the most frightful of the epidemics that hit Cincinnati as well as other big American cities during the nineteenth century. It came into Europe through Russia and hit the western world for the first time in 1830. By 1831 it had leaped across the Atlantic and had begun to attack many American communities. The first outbreak of cholera in Cincinnati occurred in the summer of 1832 and, as noted above, prompted Lyman Beecher to delay his arrival in the city. From time to time Cincinnati would again undergo the agonies that cholera inflicted. It was, as we shall see, to be an important part of Harriet's experience, and would have an intimate connection with the composition of *Uncle Tom's Cabin.*

At first sight it might not seem that a place like Cincinnati would be a particularly favorable location for a novelist to gather information for a book about slavery. Ohio was a free state in which slavery was banned by law. The land of slavery lay to the south, separated from free soil by the broad and swiftly flowing waters of the Ohio River. But outward appearances were deceptive. From the very start, slavery was intertwined with settlement in Cincinnati and made a deep impact upon all of its people.

When Ohio won statehood in 1803 a law was at once passed forbidding black people to enter the state and to soil it by their presence. The white settlers, whether they came from the North or the South, were deeply prejudiced against black people and wanted to keep them out of their communities. But for years this Ohio law remained a dead letter, and black people moved into the state just like anybody else. Almost all these black people came from the South, and most of them were ex-slaves who had either been freed by their owners or had won their freedom by purchasing it. For such people the free land north of the Ohio River was a magnet, because it was difficult if not impossible for them to go on living in the South. Many Southern states had laws not only forbidding freedmen to live there but also providing that, if caught, they might be re-enslaved. Everywhere throughout the South the free black led a bitter, segregated existence that was only one degree less odious than bondage itself.

Thus by 1833, when Harriet arrived in Cincinnati, there were three thousand black residents in the city, more than half of whom were ex-slaves. One person in ten of the city's population was black. The black people lived in "Little Africa," or the First and Fourth Wards, crowded into tinderbox shacks and vermin-ridden shanties. They performed the town's hardest and dirtiest work. Segregated and despised, unorganized and unschooled, they lacked skills and in order to live had to submit to drudgery, making and hauling bricks at the brick kilns, loading and unloading boats at the docks, toiling in the slaughter-houses. The women for the most part were in household service. Many of these people, in addition, used part of their scanty earnings to buy the freedom of other members of their families—husbands, wives, and children—who were still being held as slaves someplace in the South.

A number of these black migrants from the South were successful not only in buying freedom for themselves and their families but also in settling on the land and beginning to earn their living as farmers. Lane Seminary during the 1830s divided some of its estate into small lots and rented these to black tenants. In later years, Harriet, burdened by a growing family, would turn to these families for household help. From these black women who came into her home she would absorb, during the long hours of work in and around the house, endless details about the life of people under slavery, and about the slave system itself. "Time would fail me," she wrote to her friend Eliza Follen shortly after the publication of *Uncle Tom's Cabin,* "to tell you all that I learned incidentally of the slave system, in the history of various slaves who came into my family. . . ."

Cincinnati was not only a magnet for ex-slaves, it was a haven also for runaways. Throughout the time of Harriet's Cincinnati residence Southern newspapers were, week after week, crammed with advertisements describing the men, women, and children who had run away. Runaways were described by sex, age, weight, clothing, speech, color of skin and hair, and above all by the mutilations or scars they bore. During the Cincinnati years Harriet would read literally hundreds of these advertisements printed in the papers or posted up in prominent places such as country stores or steamboat landings. Here is a notice typical of those that Harriet would read, collect, and eventually publish:

$200 REWARD

RAN AWAY . . . On the 23rd of June last a bright mulatto woman, named Julia, about 25 years of age. She is of common size, nearly white, and very likely. She may attempt to pass for white, dresses fine. She took with her Anna, her child, 8 or 9 years old, and considerably darker than her mother. I will give a reward of $200, if caught in any Free State, and put in any good jail in Kentucky or Tennessee, so I can get them.

Nashville, Tennessee   A. W. Johnson

In the border states of Tennessee, Kentucky, and Virginia black people were tempted to play for the high stakes of total release from slavery. Thousands of them fled the South in this way between 1800 and 1860. Many passed through Cincinnati, which by 1830 had become the central link in the western freedom trails that led from slave territory to final security in Canada. Bitter struggles broke out on free soil when the fugitives were pursued by owners who sought to seize them and drag them back to bondage. Harriet, during the Cincinnati years, would hear many stirring tales of such struggles, and she and her family would play their own part in giving help to runaways fleeing northward. "We have never shrunk from the fugitives," she wrote proudly in 1851 to the famous black antislavery leader, Frederick Douglass, "and we have helped them with all we had to give."

Cincinnati's black population, then, was a southern population whose experience and memory of slavery was vivid, recent, and direct. Harriet, when she came to Cincinnati, came to a place on the borders of the slave empire which provided many opportunities for the study of the slavery system and its impact upon the lives of the millions of black people who endured it.

The Western Female Institute opened in the spring of 1833. Mary Dutton, much to Harriet's joy, came west and joined the school. Soon the hard work of teaching was absorbing all of Harriet's energies. As she herself put it, "my whole time has been taken up with the labor of our new school, or wasted in the fatigue and lassitude following such labor."

As she followed this often dull routine somber thoughts must have passed through Harriet's mind. How soon Catharine's rosy visions had vanished into air, giving way to the same painful and loveless reality that Harriet had experienced in Hartford! Would she ever succeed, as women were supposed to, in finding a man, getting married, and having a career of taking care of a husband and raising a family? Or was she doomed to remain always unmarried, a spinster? Would she become in just a few years somebody like Catharine, or, if she tired of teaching, like Aunt Esther who gave her life to running her brother's household and helping to take care of his children?

Harriet had come to Cincinnati because even though she was now an adult, she had no life of her own, no real independence outside of her family. When Lyman and Catharine made the decision, Harriet followed passively along. Even in her writing, at that time, she was still much under the domination of her older sister. Since the middle of 1832 Harriet had been working diligently on her children's geography; and, by the time the Western Female Institute opened, the work was ready for the press. It was published in May 1833. The writing was all Harriet's own, Catharine had contributed nothing. But the publisher's advertisement announced *A New Geography for Children* by Catharine E. Beecher.

We do not know how Harriet accepted this insult to her creative work, but it is likely that she swallowed the humiliation without protest. Who was she, after all, but the insignificant younger sister of that great educator Catharine Beecher?

During the summer of 1833 there was time for relaxation before the fall term began. Mary Dutton had been invited to visit the home of one of her pupils who lived in Washington, Kentucky, and she took Harriet along with her on the trip. They went by steamboat down the Ohio to Maysville, and then rode by stagecoach the dozen or so miles to Washington. There were plantations within easy ride of the little village where Mary and Harriet stayed; the two of them with their hosts must have taken enjoyable trips exploring the Kentucky countryside. Harriet did not leave any record of her impressions on this, her first contact with the land of slavery; but it is clear that she absorbed a great deal and stored it away for future use. "In reading *Uncle Tom's Cabin*," Mary wrote many years later, "I recognized scene after scene of that visit portrayed with the minutest fidelity, and knew at once where the material for that portion of the story had been gathered."

In the late summer of 1833, when Harriet and Mary had returned from Kentucky, the students began to arrive at Lane for the first academic year that would open under Lyman's leadership. There were nearly one hundred young men, all of them college graduates, most of them in their late twenties or early thirties. Among them was one,

Theodore Weld from Connecticut, whom many already acknowledged as their leader.

Theodore Weld was born in 1803 in Hampton, Connecticut, the son of a Congregational minister. When he grew up he experienced a religious conversion and was fired with the desire to save souls and to reform the world. He championed a variety of causes, including temperance and crafts education; and he roamed across the country lecturing to people and spreading his ideas. By 1833 he had come to the conclusion that the most urgent reform to be undertaken in America was the abolition of slavery. This, he believed, as a disciple of Garrison, must be started at once, and must be carried through if possible without the use of violence.

Weld had decided, too, by this time that he must become a minister. Fired with a vision of the future greatness of the West, he had selected Lane Seminary as the ideal place to complete his education in theology. He thought of Lane, too, not only as a center for Christian education but as a place from which to bring the spirit of reform, and above all the antislavery cause, to the West.

Weld made a tremendous impression upon people who met him. They came under a personal spell that was almost magical. His hair was tousled and dark, and his eyes were black and piercing. His face, with its deeply etched lines and bushy eyebrows, was almost frightening in its gravity; it had, as one observer put it, "the severity of a streak of lightning." Weld's voice was rich and mellow, and he could without apparent effort make himself heard even in a large hall. But he was not a cold person; his personal charm was considerable, and people found the warmth of his smile haunting.

Weld had scarcely arrived at Lane in August 1833 when the college was hit by an outbreak of cholera; in the first three days thirty of the one hundred students became sick, and three died.

In this crisis Weld took over the leadership of the student body. He showed by his own personal example how a Christian person ought to behave in such a situation— ready to give up everything, even life itself, for his brothers and sisters. He nursed the sick himself and shared their agonies. When students died he was with them at the end. He organized the care of the sick by converting the college into a hospital where the students provided nursing services, cooked food for the invalids, heated and carried water, prepared bandages, and gave out medicines. For a period of ten days he was on the go day and night, inspiring others with his own courage and doing without sleep for as long as forty-eight hours at a stretch.

Once the battle against cholera was over and won, Weld returned to his plans to convert the student body to the abolition cause. Most of the Lane students, at that time, were hostile to the idea of abolition or, at best, indifferent. Weld accordingly made careful preparations early in 1834 for a discussion of the issue on campus. He set up a student antislavery committee and launched a series of debates which took place in the Seminary Hall during the month of February.

Night after night, for eighteen nights, the students gathered to discuss the problem of slavery and to listen to speakers of differing viewpoints. Lyman Beecher himself urged upon them the cause of "colonization." This was the doctrine that black people were not, and could never become, American citizens; and that, when freed, they must be deported back to Africa where they would form new communities or black "colonies." This, said Lyman, was a very expensive process and in any event could only take place very slowly.

Theodore Weld, on the other hand, put forward the position of William Lloyd Garrison, that black people are indeed American citizens, that it is a crime to enslave them, that the process of liberation must begin at once. Southern students, some of them sons of plantation owners, rose to tell of their own experiences with slavery, and of the cruelties they had witnessed. James Bradley, Lane's only black student, held everybody spellbound as he told how he had been brought to the United States on a slave ship when he was a little boy, how he had been sold to an owner in Arkansas, and how he had finally purchased his freedom.

The result of the Lane debates was that the student body became converted to Garrisonian views and to the antislavery cause. The students set up at the Seminary an Antislavery Society to help make antislavery views known throughout the Midwest. Cincinnati felt the impact of this decision at once. The Lane Antislavery Society undertook to provide for the education of the entire black community of the city.

Theodore Weld and the Lane students launched their educational project in April 1834, just one year after Catharine Beecher had started the Western Female Institute. Weld's school, unlike Catharine's, was open to black people of all ages and both sexes. There were lectures on science and literature three or four times a week, and there were classes every night for adults who wanted to learn to read and write. There were Bible classes on Sundays. Two Lane students ran the school, working full time, and many Lane students gave their services on a part-time basis. Five young women—Phebe Mathews, Emeline Bishop, Susan Lowe, Lucy Wright, and Mary Ann Fletcher—came out from New York to teach the women and children.

All of this educational work took place in the ghetto, in Little Africa. The Lane students stayed overnight in homes there, and the black people on their side came out to Walnut Hills to consult with their instructors. For the first time in the history of Cincinnati black and white people were to be seen in the street arm in arm.

All of this seemed to the students like perfectly natural and Christian behavior. Lyman Beecher and members of his faculty, on the other hand, were shocked. Beecher had many talks with Weld and urged him again and again to go slow with this integration business. Setting up schools, said Lyman, was one thing; mingling with black people in the ghetto was quite another. "If you visit with colored families and walk with them in the streets," he warned Weld, "you will be overwhelmed." The angry and impassioned arguments lasted well into the night.

As for the Lane Board of Trustees, they were outraged. They had set up a college to help reclaim white souls in the wilderness, not to agitate for the abolition of slavery and for equal rights for black people. They looked upon Theodore Weld and the students who followed him as the wildest of revolutionaries. All the influential people of Cincinnati agreed with them; Lane Seminary had become a menace to be dreaded even more than cholera itself. Popular disapproval, too, was expressed in outbursts of mob violence directed against the ghetto schools. People began to refer to Lane Seminary as "that abolition hole."

And so the Board of Trustees took quick action. In August 1834, when the students were away for the summer, and Lyman Beecher was in the East raising money, they simply abolished the Lane Antislavery Society. New school regulations were set forth that ruled out

> any public meetings or discussions among the students, any public addresses by the students in the Seminary or elsewhere, or appeals or communications to the students at their meals or when assembled on other ordinary occasions, without the approbation of the faculty.

The abolition of the Lane Antislavery Society automatically destroyed the students' educational project in the ghetto, which was organized, conducted, and financed by the Society.

When Lyman Beecher came back to Lane in October 1834 he did not resign his position in protest against this suppression of freedom of speech, nor did he protest in any other way against the new regulations. On the contrary, he, along with Calvin Stowe, Professor of Biblical Literature at the Seminary, drew up a statement in support of the Trustees' action. Weld, said Beecher, must bear the blame for the whole situation. His "monomania" about slavery had threatened the survival of the Seminary.

Harriet, like everybody else in Walnut Hills, knew Theodore Weld. She saw him not only at the Seminary but also at her father's church. But Weld's thought and personality did not yet have very much impact upon her; in 1834 she was still observing the antislavery scene in rather a detached way, from a distance. Harriet at the time was totally absorbed in her work at the Female Institute in downtown Cincinnati, and it would have been hard for her to have come closer to the student movement. Nor did Harriet condemn her father for his part in the whole affair. Catharine, as much as Lyman, continued to be vehement in her disapproval of Theodore Weld and the Lane "incendiaries." For Harriet, the time was still in the future when she would declare her independence and part company, as far as her antislavery views were concerned, with the dominating figures in her life.

The results of the Board of Trustees' action and of Beecher's surrender to their will were disastrous. The majority of the students, including Weld, quit the college. Antislavery opinion began to condemn Lane as a new Bastille, a stronghold of dictatorship. Wealthy benefactors like Arthur and Lewis Tappan of New York at once withdrew much of their financial support. Almost no new students came to replace the ones who had left. Between 1836 and 1840 the college was graduating only five students a year on the average.

Thus within two short years of his arrival at Cincinnati Lyman Beecher's fortunes had received a deadly blow. He was fifty-nine years of age. A failure even more bitter than the one he had experienced in Boston was staring him in the face.

CHAPTER FOUR

IN THE PRESENCE OF MINE ENEMIES
The Antislavery Experience, 1835–38

*Thou preparest a table before me
in the presence of mine enemies.*

—*Psalm 23*

For Harriet the first half of 1834 passed in the dull routine at the Female Institute to which she had grown accustomed. Now that her *Geography* was completed, Harriet had begun to embark on a fresh literary venture. She was contributing short stories to a new journal, *The Western Monthly Magazine,* which was launched in 1833 by a Cincinnati editor, Judge James Hall. Hall offered, in September of that year, a $50 prize for the best short story to be submitted to him. Harriet composed a tale entitled "A New England Sketch." Great was her excitement and gratification when it was announced that this tale had won the contest. It was published in the April 1834 issue of the *Western Monthly*. Harriet's success inspired her to contribute other stories to Cincinnati weekly magazines. By 1840 she had won in Ohio a firm reputation as a local writer of talent and of promise.

By 1834 Harriet's life had been enriched by the discovery of a new friend in the person of Eliza Stowe, wife of Calvin Ellis Stowe, Lane's Professor of Biblical Literature. This friendship was a great delight to her. She described Eliza Stowe as "a delicate pretty little woman, with hazel eyes, auburn hair, fair complexion, fine color, a pretty little mouth, fine teeth, and a most interesting simplicity of manner; I fell in love with her directly."

In the summer of that year Harriet went back east to attend her brother Henry Ward's graduation from Amherst College in Massachusetts. While she was away, cholera hit Walnut Hills once more, and one of its victims was Eliza Stowe. When Eliza died in early August the whole Lane community mourned for her. For Harriet it was a sudden and bitter blow.

Eliza's death brought Harriet and Calvin Stowe together. They were two lonely people united by a common sense of loneliness and loss. Like Harriet, Calvin Stowe was a New Englander. Nine years older than she, he had been born in Natick, Massachusetts, the son of the village baker. Calvin's father died when the boy was very young, and he was apprenticed to a papermaker. But Calvin Stowe was clearly both intelligent and academically talented; somehow the funds were raised to send him to school. Graduating from Bowdoin College in Maine in 1824, he came to Lane in 1831 as one of the most outstanding biblical scholars of his generation.

Calvin, like Harriet, was a studious and hardworking person; he also had a fine sense of humor and an endless supply of New England yarns that Harriet never tired of listening to. He shared with her a fondness for books and a talent for writing. Both of them were members of the Semi-Colon Club, a literary group that met regularly every week to read their compositions to each other. On one occasion Calvin fascinated the audience with a perfectly serious account of all the apparitions and phantoms by which he was surrounded, and which had been appearing to him since he was a boy. Some of these were terrifying creatures, real monsters. But one of them was a pleasant character called Harvey, with whom Calvin had always been on the best of terms. "He was a great favorite of mine," Calvin told the Semi-Colon Club, "for though we neither of us spoke, we perfectly understood, and were entirely devoted to each other."

During the winter of 1834 Harriet went with Calvin and her father to the annual assembly of the Ohio Protestant churches, which was held at Ripley in October. Their host was the Reverend John Rankin, who lived in a little house on a high bluff overlooking the Ohio River.

Reverend Rankin, himself a Southerner, originally from Tennessee, was an agent in what has become known to history as the "Underground Railroad." This was an informal network of antislavery people who took in fugitive slaves, sheltered and fed them, provided them with medical attention if they were wounded or exhausted, and then sent them on. Every night Rankin hung a lighted lantern in his window as a beacon to guide runaways to his home.

The road to freedom was not called "underground" because it had hidden tunnels, or anything of that sort, but because its agents were obliged to work in secret. People like Rankin were acting in direct defiance of a federal law—the Fugitive Slave Act of 1793—which made it an offense to take in runaways, to shelter them from their pursuers, or to give them any kind of aid. Anyone convicted of these things could be punished with a heavy fine.

The Fugitive Slave Act also recognized the right of slaveholders to seize their slaves wherever they found them and drag them back into bondage. There was thus no place in the entire United States where black fugitives could be safe. Even when they had crossed the Ohio River to free soil they must always flee northward until they reached Canada where British law protected them from arrest and from return to the land of slavery.

The Reverend John Rankin was famous in antislavery circles because he was the first person in Ohio to befriend and give aid to a fugitive black woman called Eliza Harris. Eliza Harris' experience was the most thrilling of many stories about heroic runaways that Rankin told the Beecher party during their visit.

Eliza Harris was a young slave woman who lived on a plantation in Kentucky, several miles south of the Ohio River. Her husband lived on a neighboring estate. One child was left to her of three who had been born. The other two had died.

One day Eliza found out that her owners, having fallen into debt, had decided to sell her and the child, but to different buyers. She resolved at once to make her escape, and fled with her child toward the river—it was March, the waters were still frozen, and she expected to be able to cross without difficulty.

Eliza reached the river's edge after walking all night. To her dismay she found that a thaw had set in; the ice, broken up into huge blocks, was drifting downstream. For a whole day she lingered on the bank, hoping to find some way to cross. As night fell she saw her pursuers, slave catchers mounted on horses and with a pack of dogs, drawing near. With the courage of despair she determined to cross over on the ice or to die in the attempt. Holding her child tightly with one hand, leaping, scrambling, and sliding from block to block, she crossed the river on the slippery, heaving ice.

A man standing on the Ohio side of the river watched Eliza's progress. Deeply moved at the spectacle of her heroism and her despair, he helped her up the riverbank, half paralyzed as she was with cold, and directed her to Rankin's house with its shining lantern. Rankin took Eliza and the child in, nursed them back to health, and sent them on to the next "station," or shelter, on the underground line.

Harriet's interest in the Underground Railroad was now thoroughly aroused. She plied Reverend Rankin with questions and learned more about it. Rankin told her about Catharine and Levi Coffin, who lived in Newport, Indiana, and were already known throughout the Midwest for the work that they did in aid of fugitives.

Levi Coffin was born in 1798 in North Carolina, a member of a Quaker family that lived on Nantucket Island before settling in the South. Coffin moved to Newport, Indiana, in 1825; caring for black runaways, and giving whatever help to them he could, became the central purpose of his life. In this work his wife was an enthusiastic partner. When the Coffins moved to Cincinnati in 1847, they had given help, by their own estimate, to two thousand fugitives; and Coffin had won, for his unselfish labors, the title of "president" of the Underground Railroad. In all these years, Coffin recalled,

seldom a week passed without our receiving passengers. . . . We knew not what night or what hour of the night we would be aroused from slumber by a gentle rap at the door. . . . Outside in the cold or rain, there would be a two-horse wagon loaded with fugitives, perhaps the greater part of them women and children. I would invite them, in a low tone, to come in, and they would follow me into the darkened house without a word, for we knew not who might be watching or listening. When they were all safely inside and the door fastened, I would cover the windows, strike a light and build a good fire.

There was much for the Coffins to do when these people, cold, hungry, and often sick, arrived. They and the horses had to be fed, beds and blankets found. Many runaways came in shivering and in rags or barefoot. Clothing had to be collected from neighbors and well-wishers, money raised for the purchase of shoes. Those sick or close to collapse from exhaustion had to be nursed back to health before being sent on.

During her own residence in Cincinnati Harriet would

have the opportunity, from her own experience of the Underground Railroad, to satisfy herself of the truth of what Rankin had told her about the heroism and the sufferings of the runaways, and the courage of the antislavery workers, both black and white, who defied the law to help them. Eliza Harris' struggle for freedom and the selfless work of the Coffins—who in the novel she renamed Rachel and Simeon Halliday—would be immortalized in *Uncle Tom's Cabin*.

After the Beechers had come back from Ripley, Calvin gave a series of lectures upon learned subjects from the pulpit of Lyman Beecher's Second Presbyterian Church. Harriet attended these lectures regularly, and reported them for the Cincinnati *Journal*. She, of course, showed Calvin her write-ups before she sent them in. The two spent pleasant hours going over and correcting what she had written. Calvin proposed to her in August 1835, and they were married in the first week of January 1836.

Calvin was short and roly-poly, with thinning hair, and very much the absentminded professor. Harriet was extremely proud of his talents as a scholar and public speaker—"my old Rabbi," she used to call him. She now moved into Calvin's faculty residence at Walnut Hills, and for the first time in her life had a home of her very own.

The pleasant new life at Walnut Hills was soon interrupted by the demands of Calvin's job. Lane Seminary sent him on a trip to Europe in the spring of 1836 to gather books for the school library. In addition he had a grant from the State of Ohio to study foreign educational methods and to write a report. So in May, Professor Stowe went away and Harriet was once more alone. For the time that her husband was gone she went back to her father's house to live; and now she was pregnant.

The first two years of Harriet's married life, from 1836 to 1838, were crucial for her intellectual development and for the awakening of her interest in the slavery question. Up until then she had been too busy with teaching school to give her full attention to anything else. But the hard unending work of teaching was now behind her. She had time to look around, to read and to reflect. Now, in her own time and in her own way, she began to move toward the conclusion that if slavery was contrary to the law of God, as she knew it was, then the abolition of slavery must be God's will. Action against slavery, in other words, was the most pressing duty that a Christian person in America could undertake.

The first experience that moved Harriet toward this conclusion was the struggle that developed in Cincinnati in 1836 around James Gillespie Birney and his newspaper, *The Philanthropist*.

James Gillespie Birney was the son of a wealthy Kentucky slaveholder and aristocrat. In 1816, when he was a young man, Birney was attracted by the possibility of making money from the production of cotton, which at that time was starting to sweep across the South. He married Agatha McDowell, a member of a prominent Kentucky family, moved with his bride to Alabama, purchased a plantation and brought together a gang of black slaves.

But Birney did not do very well in the cotton-raising business. Hard times, lavish spending, and inexperience proved to be his ruin. By 1832 he was thinking of leaving the South altogether. He and Agatha had six sons, and four of these still had to be put through college. Perhaps, the Birneys thought to themselves, they ought to settle down at Jacksonville, Illinois; there was a fine college there headed by the well-known Edward Beecher. This, they felt sure, could provide a good education for their sons.

Birney was anxious to educate his sons in the North because by this time he had abandoned not only his taste for growing cotton but also the proslavery ideas of his youth. He was at first attracted by the program of the colonizationists who believed that while black people ought to be liberated, they could never become American citizens and would have to be shipped back to Africa. But Birney soon abandoned such ideas and moved forward toward Garrisonian convictions. The Lane debates of February 1834, which he followed through reports in antislavery journals, were a key factor in his conversion. In the spring of 1834 he visited Walnut Hills to talk with Theodore Weld; and Weld made the same profound impression upon Birney as he did upon so many other people.

This visit to Walnut Hills marked the final stage in Birney's conversion to thoroughgoing abolitionism. He resigned from the Colonization Society, of which he was an agent, freed the last of the slaves remaining in his possession, and issued a public statement explaining the reasons for his decision. This statement was distributed throughout the South by Lane students. That a Southerner born and bred, a slaveholder and an aristocrat, should champion the doctrines of the antislavery cause—here indeed was news!

In order to encourage debate about slavery, Birney decided to return to his native Kentucky and to launch an antislavery newspaper there. But the opposition of Kentucky slaveholders to this move was so fierce that Birney was obliged to abandon the project. He decided instead to make Cincinnati, Queen City of the West, a center for the diffusion of antislavery ideas. In October 1835, just one year after Theodore Weld had been obliged to leave, Birney bought a home in Cincinnati and prepared to move his family in. He gathered a small group of antislavery people around him, founded the Ohio Antislavery Society, and launched a new antislavery newspaper, *The Philanthropist.* The first number was published on January 1, 1836, the same week that Harriet was married.

The leading people of Cincinnati—merchants, doctors, clergymen, and lawyers—reacted to Birney just as they had to Theodore Weld and the Lane Student Antislavery Society, with frenzied hostility. At the end of January 1836 these people called a public meeting with the mayor of Cincinnati, Samuel Davies, in the chair. In speech after speech Birney was denounced as a firebrand and a rebel; he was a threat to the Constitution and the Union; he must either be silenced or driven out.

But Birney did not back down before these threats. First he stood up in the crowded meeting itself, before the angry audience, demanded his right to be heard, and spoke in defense of his ideas. And then he made an even bolder move. Until April *The Philanthropist* was printed in the little town of Richmond, twenty miles outside of Cincinnati. Birney now moved the entire publishing operation into the very heart of the city. He would defend the right to print his paper and to express his views in the capital of the Midwest itself.

Cincinnati's leaders had no intention of tolerating such defiance. On July 12 a mob of white men broke into Birney's printing press and scattered the type. Handbills were posted at street corners, warning that if the press were started up again, worse punishment would follow. "Abolitionists Beware!" ran the leaflet; "if an attempt is made to reestablish the press, it will be viewed as an act of defiance to an already outraged community. On the heads of the abolitionists will be the results which will follow."

Birney's answer to this warning was clear and bold, and he published it in *The Philanthropist* on July 22. "Must we trample on the liberty of *white* men here," he asked, "because slaveholders have trampled on the liberty of *Black* men at the South? Must we forge chains for the *mind* here, because they have forged them for the *body* there? Must we extinguish the right to *speak,* the right to *print* in the North, that we may be in unison with the South? No, never!"

As for Birney's family, they went to bed at night in fear of their lives, listening for any sound that might warn of a coming attack, and with their muskets ready. But the press continued to operate, and *The Philanthropist* continued to come out.

By this time Calvin Stowe had arrived in Europe, and Harriet wrote to tell her husband all about this new antislavery crisis in Cincinnati. It was almost certain, she wrote, that the mob would attack Birney's office again; and this time they would destroy the press itself. As for herself, she proudly declared that she was ready to join with Birney and the Ohio Antislavery Society in their freedom fight. "My sympathies," she told Calvin, "are strongly enlisted for Mr. Birney, and I hope that he will stand his ground and assert his rights. His office is fireproof and enclosed in high walls. I wish he would man it with armed men and see what can be done. If I were a man I would go, for one, and take care of one window."

At this time Harriet contributed unsigned short articles to the Cincinnati *Journal*, a weekly magazine that her brother Henry Ward was editing temporarily while its chief editor was out of town. She warned of the dangers of mob rule and of permitting any violation of the rights of private citizens. "I thought," she wrote to Calvin, "that I was, like a good wife, defending one of your principles in your absence, and wanted you to see how manfully I talked about it." Harriet's and Henry Ward's voices were almost the only ones raised publicly in Cincinnati to condemn the destruction of Birney's press. Almost all the other papers in town kept their silence or supported the action of the mob.

Harriet was not yet a person with antislavery convictions as strong as those of Garrison or Weld; but she believed that the abolitionists, like everybody else, had the right to state their views and to make them known. She saw that Birney and his friends were ready if necessary to lay down their lives for this right. She viewed their struggle and their courage with sympathy and admiration. She had now taken a big step forward from the seeming indifference with which she had reacted to the Board of Trustees' suppression of freedom of speech at Lane Seminary in 1834.

On July 23, the very next day after Birney's refusal to

abandon his right to publish, Cincinnati leaders called a public meeting, demanded that *The Philanthropist* cease publication at once, and warned that this demand would be enforced if necessary with violence. One week later a mob gathered at the Exchange Hotel and decided upon its order of business—first to destroy the press and then to lynch Birney. When the sun went down the crowd rushed to *The Philanthropist* office and broke down the door. Books, type, printing metal, and office furniture were tossed out the windows and smashed or splintered in the street outside. When the office was a total wreck, the printing press was pushed out, dragged down the street and thrown into the river.

Then the rioters went to Birney's house, but did not find him home. Instead they invaded Little Africa and vented their fury upon the homes and persons of innocent black people. Windows were smashed, doors ripped off their hinges, houses broken into and left a shambles, while the terrified inhabitants fled for their lives down the alleys.

The mayor of Cincinnati looked on quietly while the mob ran wild. Finally he stepped in to curb the racist frenzy. Volunteer companies were organized to patrol the streets. Henry Ward Beecher, then a student at Lane, joined one of these companies, whose job it was to protect the Seminary from an expected invasion by the rioters. As her brother went off in the morning to join the patrol, two pistols strapped to his belt, Harriet was frightened for his safety; but her heart also swelled with pride.

Early in August of 1836 the city was calm again. Birney brought in a new press and went on publishing *The Philan-*

thropist as though nothing had happened. But now Harriet was keenly interested to learn exactly what it was the abolitionists were saying that aroused so much anger and controversy. She began for the first time to read *The Philanthropist* and to absorb its antislavery views. She made friends with the newspaper's assistant editor, Dr. Gamaliel Bailey, who had once taught physiology at Lane and who took over the job of editor-in-chief in 1837.

Harriet also thought deeply about the meaning of Birney's struggle for the right to publish his views. Slavery, it was becoming clear to her, was more than just a physical fact—the fact, that is, that some people owned other people and could bind them with chains. No, slavery was also an American institution whose law and power were realities extending far beyond the borders of the South itself. The silence of freeborn Americans was enforced, in the case of Lane students in 1834, with legal regulations and the threat of expulsion. In Birney's case it was clear that the slavery interests could also call upon violence to stifle discussion.

Toward the end of September, while Calvin was still in Germany, Harriet gave birth to twin girls. Calvin did not know he had become a father until he landed in New York in January 1837. Harriet wanted one of the children named after Eliza Stowe, and Calvin insisted that the other twin be named after her own mother. And so they were christened Eliza and Harriet.

From this time on Mrs. Stowe was very busy with the care of her daughters. But she also found time to follow carefully yet another battle around the freedom of the press

that was fought in Illinois and that involved her brother
Edward and his close friend Elijah Lovejoy.

Elijah Lovejoy was a New Englander and the son of a
Congregational minister. Born on a farm in Albion,
Maine, in 1802, he was graduated from Waterville College
in 1826 at the top of his class. Lovejoy, like so many other
dedicated young men at that time, was fascinated by the
romance of the West and by the possibilities of Christian
service there. He settled in St. Louis, Missouri, and in
1833 launched a newspaper there, *The Observer,* devoted to
"Christian politics, diffusion of religious information, and
the saving of souls."

The first things that Elijah Lovejoy wrote about were
not so very earthshaking—things like temperance and the
importance of reading the Bible. But this did not last for
long. In 1834 Lovejoy met Andrew Benton, a Missourian
who was secretary of the Lane Student Antislavery Society,
and Benton told him about the Lane debates. By 1835
Lovejoy was moving in the direction of Garrisonian convictions.

Now *The Observer* began to tackle the question of slavery
in earnest. Slavery, wrote Lovejoy, is a crime against God.
God, in His own time, will punish the people who are
guilty of such cruel oppression. Liberation of the slaves
must begin at once, must go forward peacefully but with
deliberate speed.

The reaction of white people in St. Louis to Lovejoy's
writings was the same as that of white people in Cincinnati
to Birney's. The city's newspapers unleashed a campaign
against Lovejoy; community leaders organized mass meet-

ings to mobilize opinion against him. So Lovejoy left the hate-ridden city for a breathing spell in the summer of 1835 and went to Jacksonville College to attend the commencement exercises. He talked with Edward Beecher; the two men found that they were at one in their views on slavery and the importance of defending the right to a free press.

Strengthened by Beecher's support, Lovejoy went back to St. Louis for the ordeal that lay ahead of him. It was clear that a violent attack upon *The Observer*'s office was only a matter of time.

The spark that touched off the explosion was the lynching of Frank McIntosh in April 1836. McIntosh was a black worker on the steamboat *Flora*. When his boat docked in St. Louis on April 28 he went ashore and got involved in a street brawl. The whites in the fight escaped; only the black man was arrested. The arresting officers threatened McIntosh, as they dragged him away, with a long prison term, or lashing, or both. McIntosh, in a rage, killed one of the men who had arrested him. Soon he was overpowered and taken off to jail.

When word of what had happened got around, a mob formed, took McIntosh out of the jail, chained him to a tree on the St. Louis common, and burned him to death. He pleaded frantically for someone to end his suffering with a gun. The lynchers ignored his moans.

The next day Elijah Lovejoy went to the scene, viewed the charred body, and wrote a passionate protest which he published in *The Observer*. The mob leaders were never tried for murder—an indictment against them was dismissed by Judge Lawless of the St. Louis Criminal Court. On the contrary, Lovejoy, not the lynchers, was looked upon as the culprit because he had dared to raise his voice in protest against the lynching.

This was the signal for action against *The Observer*. The mob looted Lovejoy's office first in May, then again in July.

So Lovejoy decided to leave St. Louis and to locate his press on free soil, on the other side of the Mississippi in Alton, Illinois. But scarcely had his press been delivered at the Alton wharf when a band of Missourians seized it and threw it into the river.

With the support of Illinois ministers, Lovejoy now bought a new press and began once more to publish antislavery views. The result in Alton was the same as in St. Louis. There were mass meetings, press campaigns, bitter personal attacks. In August 1837 Lovejoy's second press was destroyed; he sent for a third press, and it suffered the same fate. The mob broke it up and dumped it in the river in September, just one month later.

Edward Beecher now felt that it was time to take part in the Alton struggle. He and other Illinois ministers decided to hold an antislavery meeting at Alton to rally support around Lovejoy; the date was set for October 26, 1837.

When the time came a surprise was in store for the antislavery people. The hall was packed to overflowing with the champions of "law and order." A resolution was proposed calling upon Lovejoy to give up newspaper work as a condition for his continuing to live in the city.

Then Lovejoy got to his feet to speak against the resolution. While Edward Beecher put his head down on the table and wept, the editor of *The Observer* made, in the presence of his enemies, one of the most profound and moving pleas for human rights ever uttered upon American soil. "Why should I flee from Alton?" he asked:

Is not this a free state? When assailed by a mob at St. Louis, I came here, as to the home of freedom and the laws. The mob has pursued me here, and why should I retreat again? Where can I be safe if not here? Have I not a right to claim the protection of the laws? What more can I have in any other place? Sir, the very act of retreating will embolden the mob to follow me wherever I go. No sir; there is no way to escape the mob, but to abandon the path of duty: and that, God helping me, I will never do. . . . You may burn me at the stake, as they did McIntosh at St. Louis; or you may tar and feather me, or throw me into the Mississippi, as you have so often threatened to do; but you cannot disgrace me. I, and I alone, can disgrace myself; and the deepest of all disgrace would be at a time like this, to deny my Master by forsaking his cause.

Lovejoy spoke in vain; the resolution was passed. When Lovejoy's fourth and final press arrived by boat on November 7, he and his friends, including Edward Beecher, made arrangements to defend it, guns in hand. In this final action Lovejoy was killed by a pistol bullet from the mob.

A few weeks later Edward wrote and published a pamphlet entitled *Narrative of Riots at Alton* to tell the story of the drama at Alton and to explain its meaning to the nation. His loyalty to Lovejoy and his commitment to the cause of freedom of the press now marked him as a figure of national importance in the antislavery movement.

Edward's little book came off the press at Alton early in 1838, not long after Harriet gave birth to her third child, Henry Ellis, who was born in January of that year. She read Edward's book from cover to cover, and she read it many times. *Narrative of Riots at Alton,* indeed, is a writing of much importance in Harriet's intellectual development and her relationship to the antislavery movement.

Upon what basis, Edward asked, ought we to judge of right and wrong in the confrontation that occurred at Alton? Was Lovejoy an agent of subversion, as his enemies charged? Not at all, said Edward. He was a Christian leader trying to deal with one of the fundamental problems of the time. In so doing he was giving expression to God's will and plan in the nineteenth century for the liberation of human beings from the bonds of slavery.

God's truth, Edward went on, must be learned and obeyed. Americans, like all other people on earth, must do God's will or suffer the consequences. Edward's vision of the West as the home of a free people who had purged themselves of slavery and racism found expression in the climax of the *Narrative.* Day was dawning on the last day of Lovejoy's life; the two friends stood guard at the warehouse where the fourth *Observer* press had been landed and lodged. Edward looked out over the broad and silver-shining river, and was filled with the deepest of feelings as he thought about the future of his country. "I thought of future ages," he wrote, "and of the countless millions that should dwell on this mighty stream; and that nothing but the truth would make them free."

How do men learn truth? Edward asked. Truth is made known by discussion, and evil men will try in vain to muffle it. Suppression of truth is rebellion against God, who has made of free speech and free inquiry His instrument for the rebuilding of the world. Lovejoy's martyrdom is a warning, for America is stained by the monstrous crime of slavery. This stain must be swept away if punishment is not to fall upon a guilty nation.

Such, in 1838, was Edward's conclusion, and such was Harriet's too. Slavery was a crime against God and Christians had a duty to take action against it. But how does a woman in a provincial town, burdened with the responsibility of running a household and caring for small children, become involved in such a struggle? Harriet presented the agonizing dilemma to her husband. "No one," she told him, "can have the system of slavery brought before him without an irrepressible desire to *do* something, and what is there to be done?"

CHAPTER FIVE

A GREAT CRY IN EGYPT
Family Life, 1840–50

And there was a great cry in Egypt;
for there was not one house where
there was not one dead.

–Exodus 12:30

Between 1836 and 1848 Harriet became the mother of six children. They followed fast upon each other. Harriet and Eliza, the twins, were born in 1836, and Henry Ellis in 1838. Then came Frederick William in 1840, Georgiana May in 1843, and Samuel Charles in 1848.

Throughout this entire period Harriet was fully convinced that slavery was criminally wrong, and that it was her Christian duty to struggle for its abolition. But she was burdened with frequent pregnancies, with the care of little ones, and the running of a home. When she asked Calvin, "What is there to be done about slavery?" he could give her no answer. She was tied down with her duties as mother, housekeeper, and wife. "The nursery and the kitchen," as she wrote later, "were my principal fields of labor." Some years later, when Harriet was just about to sit down and write *Uncle Tom's Cabin,* she described her life to a correspondent as "thoroughly uneventful and uninteresting."

Harriet's confinement to her home was made more total by the fact that Calvin was sometimes away for long stretches of time on college business—raising funds, recruiting students, and the like. On these occasions the management of family affairs, the supervision of the household, and the education of the children fell upon Harriet alone. In a letter to Calvin, written when he was away on a trip in 1844, she told how the entire morning, in his absence, was spent upon the children's school: "half past nine," she wrote, "call the children in to school, sing a hymn, pray with them and give them a bible lesson half an hour long. . . . They then spend half an hour on their texts and bible for Sunday. Then read in class and sew until dinner time."

Harriet called this "a private school for my own children." During the Cincinnati years, since there were no schools for black children at Walnut Hills, she admitted black pupils to her home. Many years later she recalled that one of these children failed to appear at the appointed time for school, but later she received a visit from the mother, who told a heartrending tale. "It appeared," wrote Harriet, "that the child had never been emancipated, and was one of the assets of an estate in Kentucky, and had been seized and carried off by one of the executors, and was to be sold by the sheriff at auction. . . ."

The people of Walnut Hills, including Mrs. Stowe, raised the money needed to buy the child's freedom. But, Harriet tells us, "the incident left a deep mark in my mind as to the practical workings of the institution of slavery."

All the time that the Stowes remained in Cincinnati they lived in the shadows of poverty. Economic depression hit the country in 1837, benefactors stopped giving the college money, and Lane Seminary went into debt. When the Stowes were married in 1836, Calvin's salary was $1,200 a year. By the middle 1840s he was lucky to collect even half of what was owed him. "Our straits for money," Harriet wrote in 1843, "are unparalleled . . . it seems that $600 is the very most we can hope to collect of our salary."

Thus the joys of family life and the delight of raising children were soured or blotted out by poverty and care. The struggle just to survive absorbed most of Harriet's energies. Once in a while she uttered a cry of protest and a complaint about her miserable life. "It is a dark, sloppy, rainy, muddy, disagreeable day," she wrote to Calvin in 1843, "and I have been working hard all day in the kitchen. . . . I am sick of the smell of sour milk and sour meat and sour everything and then the clothes *will* not dry and no wet thing does and everything smells mouldy; and altogether I feel as if I never wanted to eat again. . . ."

Calvin was preoccupied with his own studies and his college work. He never shared equally with Harriet the heavy responsibility of caring for the children. The sense that she bore this burden alone sometimes invaded her with crushing intensity. "You know," she pointed out to

Calvin, "except this poor head, my unfortunate household has no mainspring, for nobody feels any kind of responsibility to do a thing in time, place or manner, except as I oversee it. . . ."

The Cincinnati years wore Harriet out, physically, emotionally, and spiritually. She described herself at the end of this time as "a little bit of a woman, somewhat more than forty, about as thin and dry as a pinch of snuff; never very much to look at in my best days, and looking like a used-up article now."

All the time that Harriet lived in Cincinnati black women were coming into her home as servants to cook, to clean, and to do the washing. One of these women, Aunt Frankie, was a great comfort to her during the bleak and toil-ridden Cincinnati years. People like Aunt Frankie had been born in the South and most of them had at one time been slaves. As she worked with them in the kitchen and around the house Harriet questioned them as carefully as she had questioned the Reverend John Rankin when she was at Ripley. She learned, and she stored away in her mind, endless details about the operation of slavery and its impact upon the lives of ordinary people.

The more Harriet found out about slavery, the more intolerable it seemed to her. Both she and Calvin were strengthened in their determination to do what they could to give aid and shelter to black runaways who passed through Walnut Hills. Years later she would write in *Uncle Tom's Cabin* about fugitives whose suffering and distress she had witnessed with her own eyes.

On one occasion in 1842 nine slaves escaped from Kentucky and found refuge at Walnut Hills, where Lane students and the Stowes took care of them until they were picked up by an antislavery worker named John Van Zandt.

John Van Zandt was the owner of a beautiful farm some fifteen miles north of Walnut Hills in the township of Sharon. Here he had built for himself in 1829 a home called Mount Pierpont; and he became well known in the neighborhood for the help that he gave to fugitives. Often he would drive his wagon to market in Cincinnati, unload his produce, and carry black runaways home with him on the return trip.

On April 21, 1842, John Van Zandt picked up his "cargo" of fugitives at Walnut Hills and drove in the early morning darkness as fast as he could go along the road that led north toward Sharon. A little after daylight two or three men spotted the wagon and gave chase—they suspected that it contained runaways and hoped to win a reward for catching the black slaves and returning them to their owners. Soon they came up with the runaways and seized them—all but two who made good their escape. As for Van Zandt he was hauled into federal court and sued by the slaves' owner, Wharton Jones, for giving aid and comfort to fugitives.

The case attracted a lot of attention in the Midwest. Van Zandt defended himself with the proud statement that "it is the highest Christian duty to extend a helping hand to the poor and down-trodden . . . and the performance of such duties is the great evidence of a Christian faith." But heavy damages were awarded against him for violating the Fugitive Slave Law, and the Supreme Court of the United States itself upheld the judgment of the lower court. Van Zandt died penniless in 1848. His home Mount Pierpont along with his farm was sold to meet the execution of the court's decree.

Harriet did not forget this story of antislavery struggle and heroism. When she came to tell the story of the Underground Railroad in *Uncle Tom's Cabin,* John Van Zandt—under the name Van Tromp—would be immortalized there, along with Eliza Harris and Catharine and Levi Coffin.

Although in episodes such as this Harriet did what she could to help fugitives, she suffered from a sense of guilt because she had kept her silence about slavery and had failed to speak out against a system that she believed was criminal and wrong. This added to the pain of being poor. Poverty, for Harriet, was more than just an economic fact, because she had been taught to view it also as a punishment for sin. God, she believed, was punishing Calvin and herself because they had defied His will in remaining at Lane Seminary. Lane, as she now saw it, was an evil institution. It had placed a ban upon the discussion of slavery and it had driven away Theodore Weld and many other fine young ministers who sought through the antislavery struggle to realize God's will on earth.

Neither Harriet nor Calvin had protested this wrong. Like Lyman Beecher, they had accepted it in silence. They had gone on eating the Seminary's bread as though nothing had happened. This, surely, was a sin. Why, she asked herself, should God smile upon people who refused to listen to His voice and who by a cowardly silence gave support to evil?

The Stowes stayed at Lane Seminary until 1850, spending no less than fourteen years of their married life in a place that they both detested. Why, then, did they not leave Cincinnati much earlier?

It is certainly true that Harriet longed passionately to go back to New England and that she experienced all the bitterness and pain of an exile who longs for her native land by day and dreams about it by night. All the stories that she wrote for the Cincinnati journals, and which were published under the title of *The Mayflower* in 1843, told of life in New England; not one of them dealt with Cincinnati people.

On a visit, again, to Vermont in 1847 Harriet wrote to Calvin and told him about her feeling for the New England countryside, its pines, cypress, and evergreen laurel. She told him, too, about her yearning to be back home upon her native soil. "Oh how I wish," she exclaimed, "that you and I *lived* in such a country—I think of you all the time and scarcely enjoy anything because I pity you so much in that lonely drizzly unpleasant Cincinnati winter I know so well."

On the other hand, much as Harriet longed for New England she was also bound by strong feelings of loyalty to her father. By 1840 Lyman's second wife was dead and he had married for a third time. All the children that he had had by his first two wives were grown up, and there would be no more to come. All had left home except the youngest, James, and he too went off to college in 1843.

Lyman at that time was moving rapidly into old age. He was haunted by memories of the past and very much alone, obliged at last to live without children, as one of them put it, "to love or govern." When one or another of them came to see him he pleaded tearfully with them to stay a little longer when the time came to leave. "Tom, I love you," he told Thomas Beecher on one such occasion. "You mustn't go away and leave me. They're all gone."

In these years Lyman enjoyed the company of his terrier, Trip. He would go for walks with his little dog into the woods, and he would carry on long conversations with Trip. "Father, in those days," one of the children shrewdly observed, "found comfort venting upon Trip those tender emotions which he could not suppress nor his own children any longer receive."

Harriet, too, received these desperate pleas from the old man, not to go away and leave him. It was hard for her to resist. She was bound not only by a sense of duty but by feelings of love. To have abandoned her father in hard times would have been for Harriet like abandoning a ship and its captain in time of peril. "It was thought on all hands," she wrote later, "that we must not leave the position, but struggle on with what hope we might, til Lane Seminary should be clear from debt. It was the hardest trial of our life, at this time. . . ."

The question of whether to stay in Cincinnati or to quit produced an often bitter running debate between Harriet and her husband. Her iron determination not to abandon her father was something that Calvin found difficult to accept. He had good professional reasons of his own for wishing to find another job. One of the foremost biblical scholars of his time, Calvin was wasting his life teaching at an institution which during the late thirties and early forties was graduating only a handful of students every year. To make matters worse, he was obliged to spend long months away from his family and his beloved books in the struggle to raise funds and to recruit students. "This work," he burst out to Harriet on one occasion, "is beyond measure irksome and trying to me and the long absence from you and the children almost insupportable."

In May 1844 Calvin left for a trip to the East to raise money as the college's agent. He left home in a resigned mood, willing to accept, at least for the moment, his wife's unchanging decision. "I feel," he wrote to her at the beginning of the tour, "that I must and cannot leave Lane College for any consideration. . . . In my present state of mind your views appear to me more correct than my own have been."

But Calvin was not cut out to be a fund raiser. Two months of failure and rebuff produced in him feelings of keen frustration and drove him to despair. His mood now changed. "Unless," he told his wife at the end of July, "we can live at Walnut Hills without taking boarders or going on agency [that is, making fund-raising trips] we must leave. Now fix that definitely in your mind."

Taking in boarders was one of the ways that Harriet had tried to make a little extra money. By 1844 eight people in addition to the family were living in the house: seven of these were "paying guests" and one was a housekeeper. Harriet thus bore the responsibility for running a boardinghouse that contained fifteen people in all, including the baby, Georgiana May.

In all her experience of poverty, keeping boarders was the thing that Harriet detested most. There were the daily time-consuming trips to market to buy food; and there were the complaints about that food when it had been prepared and cooked. The boarders indulged in bickerings and quarrels among themselves, and they complained about each other—to Harriet. She was always having to listen to these complaints and having to make peace between these people if she could. Then there were the constant comings and goings and the constant ringing of the doorbell when visitors came, and the total absence of privacy. Not everybody paid their bills on time, and then Harriet had to dun her "guests."

For Harriet, a far more pleasant way of adding to the family income was by writing a sketch now and then for one of the Cincinnati journals. By 1843, when *The Mayflower* was published, she enjoyed a good reputation among Cincinnatians as an author. Calvin, in particular, prized Harriet's writings, and encouraged her to embark upon a serious literary career. "My dear," he told her in 1842, "you must be a literary woman. It is so written in the book of fate. Make your calculations accordingly. There is no woman like you in this wide world. Who else has so much talent with so little self-conceit?"

During these years Harriet did indeed dream of a literary career from which she might make enough money to support the family in comfort. But this dream was never to be realized while the Stowes remained in Cincinnati. She had, in the first place, no room of her own where she could write in peace and quiet. She was obliged to do her creative work in the children's nursery; it was impossible to concentrate as the children romped and yelled and played and Anna, the nurse, washed and dressed and fed them. And then, too, Harriet's conscience pricked her. Was it right, she asked herself, to take time to pursue her personal literary ambition with this growing family around her that needed her help and attention so much?

During these years, when Harriet was so preoccupied with her duties as housewife and mother, her concern about slavery was becoming always more intense. She reared her family against a backdrop of mounting political crisis. In 1845 Congress declared the Mexican province of Texas to be a part of the Union; war with Mexico followed and ended with a complete U.S. victory. The defeated country was obliged in 1848 to give up at sword's point the whole northern part of its territory. The United States thus seized a vast stretch of land lying between the Rio Grande and the Pacific.

Slaveholders in 1848 were casting greedy eyes on this newly won empire, which included the rich Spanish province of California; and they were talking openly about quitting the Union and taking up arms if they were not allowed to take their slaves with them into these Spanish lands. Slavery, Harriet told herself, was advancing remorselessly across the American land. But she was doing nothing about it! She was doing nothing except counting spoons, minding children, and hanging out the clothes to dry.

From the contemplation of the uselessness of her life

there came to Harriet deepening feelings of guilt and sorrow. My soul, she wrote to her brother Thomas in 1845, "longs to be at peace with God, but this cannot be! I am pinned down with a weight of cares that seems to hold me prostrate on earth."

The conflict in Harriet's soul between duty to family and duty to God expressed itself in physical illness. After Georgiana May was born in 1843 she remained an invalid for months. She complained of splitting headaches, pains in her eyes, a feeling of extreme weakness that made it useless to attempt work. At times she felt so blue that she could only sit and gaze out the window with the tears streaming down her face.

Harriet, in truth, was more than once on the verge of nervous breakdown. She talked earnestly to Calvin about going to Brattleboro in Vermont and taking the water cure that seemed to work wonders in cases like hers. Somehow—it is not clear exactly how—Calvin found ways to make known to friends and well-wishers the existence of "illness in my family," to cope with which he needed financial help. Funds began to trickle in not only from Cincinnati but from other parts of the country as well.

So in the spring of 1846 Harriet went off to a Brattleboro sanitarium to spend a year away from the cares of her family and the burdens of her household.

It was a year of liberation for Harriet, and a fresh, more carefree, life began. "For this week," she wrote to Calvin,

I have gone before breakfast to the wave-bath and let all the waves and billows roll over me till every limb ached with cold and my hands would scarcely have feeling enough to dress me. After that I have walked till I was warm, and come home to breakfast with such an appetite! Brown bread and milk are luxuries indeed, and the only fear is that I may eat too much. At eleven comes my douche, to which I have walked in a driving rain for the last two days, and after it walked in the rain again till I was warm.

Harriet was free of responsibilities, with no servants to oversee, no children to run after, no boarders to cope with, and no husband to take care of. She met all kinds of interesting people, visited endlessly, took the waters—which meant being deliciously and sinfully idle for hours—and enjoyed the winter sports, sledding and sleigh-riding by moonlight. She ate heartily of meals which other people prepared for her.

During the year in Vermont Harriet's health improved greatly, and all the painful symptoms that she had experienced earlier vanished. She returned to Cincinnati in May 1847, after an absence of fourteen months. Soon she was pregnant once more; and soon, as we might expect, all the old aches and pains came back.

While Harriet had been away Calvin had done his best to cope both with his job at the Seminary and the care of his five small sons and daughters. Now, it was his turn to be on the edge of nervous collapse; he began to go around in a permanent and unshakable mood of black despair. But by 1848 Lane Seminary's general financial situation had begun to improve, and this meant that the college could afford to provide Calvin with a rest cure too. In June

1848, accordingly, he left for a sabbatical year at Brattle-boro. Harriet in his absence struggled on, as she had always done, to make both ends meet, to keep boarders for a little extra money, to teach the children, to do the marketing, and to run the house.

In June 1849, when Calvin had been gone just a year, cholera hit Cincinnati once again. During the long summer the terrible scenes with which people had become so familiar were repeated. Burning coals smoked in the streets to cleanse the air of "malignant vapors." In the public squares carts and wagons were pressed into service to hurry corpses in an endless procession to the burial grounds. By the end of the month more than one hundred people were dying of the plague each day.

Early in July the ministers of the city solemnly declared that the epidemic was a sign of God's anger. They advised the mayor to declare Tuesday, July 3, a day of "general fasting, humiliation and prayer."

The Protestant ministers of Cincinnati in those days understood, just as we do, that disease, including infections like cholera, are brought about by natural causes. True, they had no very exact idea as to what these natural causes were: in 1848 the very existence of bacteria and their part in causing disease was unknown. But the ministers, just the same, were well aware that something in the natural environment produced illness—it might be, they thought, want of warm, dry lodgings, or proper diet, or even a sudden heat wave.

The ministers also believed that nature was under God's control. God, they thought, could bring about a plague because He wished to "correct" sinful people for something unusually wicked that they had done. Sickness, in their opinion, was a punishment that God sent upon people who had gone astray and who had disregarded His laws. In such cases the proper action for a community to take was to fast and pray. In this way you asked Heaven to be merciful and to stop punishing you; and you showed God that you knew that you had sinned, and were sorry for what you had done.

So the Cincinnati citywide fast day took place on July 3. "One hundred and twenty burials from cholera alone yesterday," wrote Harriet to Calvin on July 4, "tomorrow and next day will witness a fresh harvest of death." One week later Harriet's own son, Samuel Charles, then eighteen months old, was taken ill. While the child fretted on his bed, Aunt Frankie, the black washerwoman, died.

Aunt Frankie was a cheerful, beautiful, and courageous black woman. Harriet described her "honest bluff black face, her long strong arms, her chest as big and stout as a barrel, and her hilarious hearty laugh." Harriet, the twins, and Anna together made the shroud. When the funeral was over, she returned home to watch at the bedside of Samuel Charles, whose turn had now come to die.

There were two full weeks of anguish and waiting before Samuel Charles died on July 26. "I have just seen him, " she wrote that day to Calvin,

> in his death agony, looking on his imploring face when I could not help or soothe nor do one thing to ease his cruel suffering, do nothing but pray in my

anguish that he might die soon. I write as though there were no sorrow like my sorrow, yet there has been in this city, as in the land of Egypt, scarce a house without its dead.

In this letter Harriet revealed her inmost soul. Speaking in the pain of loneliness and sorrow, she compared the plague in Cincinnati with the plague in ancient Egypt. The sin for which the Egyptians had been punished by the death of the firstborn in each house was Pharaoh's refusal to liberate the Jewish slaves; this was a sin laid at the door not just of one man, but of the entire people. For in every house where there were children, the oldest child lay dead.

In 1849 God had spoken in Cincinnati. His warning, that the American people must act against slavery or face destruction, was to be seen in the death that was everywhere. *And God had spoken to Harriet directly.* This was the meaning of the tiny shrouded body of her son that lay in her own home.

Six years before Samuel Charles died, Harriet's older brother George had died in the prime of life at Chillicothe, Ohio, where he was a minister. George's death shook Harriet, as she said, "like an earthquake." She had written round to all her brothers and sisters. Repent now, she urged them, and be prepared to die; you, too, may be hurried like George without a moment's warning into eternity, without even a second to prepare. "Who is to be called next?" she had asked. "Are we ready? Are we all waiting with our lamp burning?"

Now Samuel Charles, her own son, had been called, and

again Harriet asked herself, "Am *I* ready?" The answer, of course, was "no." She had neither spoken nor acted resolutely enough against slavery. She had done nothing to atone for this crime so that she could meet her God without guilt. And she remembered the words of one of her father's most famous sermons, written three years before she was born, in which he had denounced the custom of dueling as one of the most vicious evils in American life. "We are murderers," Lyman had said, "while we tolerate and reward those who commit crime."

By August the cholera had diminished in intensity. In September Calvin returned home from Vermont with the news that he had been offered a fellowship at Bowdoin College, in Brunswick, Maine. Even though the salary would be less than he was supposed to be getting at Lane, this was exciting news. The decision for Harriet was all the easier because with good times Lane Seminary was now climbing out of debt and Lyman himself was at the point of retirement.

In April 1850 Harriet left Cincinnati for the last time and traveled east to Brunswick with three of her children. Seven months pregnant, she was in haste to set up a new home where her child might be born. Calvin would follow with the rest of the family when the Lane year ended in June.

The Cincinnati years had been hard and thankless for Harriet, but they had endowed her richly. She had learned the meaning of life in America for millions of women—poverty, unceasing work, and perpetual childbearing. She had come into direct contact with black ex-slaves migrating from the South, and also with fugitives. Both what she had learned by direct contact with black people and what she had herself suffered had fitted her, more than was possible for any white male, to probe the meaning and the anguish of slavery. The antislavery movement had touched her with its struggles, and it had educated her. As a person of literary talent she had reached the important conclusion that it was her duty to God to take up her pen and to use it to help awaken the American people from an ignorance about slavery, and an indifference to it, that menaced their very survival. The literary gifts that had lain so long hidden were finally to be called forth by the nation's crisis and to be used as a weapon in the struggle against human bondage.

CHAPTER SIX

THEY SHALL BE DELIVERED UP
National Crisis, 1850

*Runaway slaves "shall be delivered
up on claim of the party to whom
such service or labor may be due."*

—U.S. Constitution, Article IV

While Harriet and her family were moving back to New England from Cincinnati during the early months of 1850, the United States was in the grip of a political crisis. It seemed as though war between North and South was about to break out.

This crisis arose out of the conflict with Mexico that had ended with United States victory in 1848 and the surrender by Mexico of millions of acres of land. What was to be done with this conquered territory? Even during the war Northerners and Southerners had quarreled bitterly over the question of whether or not slavery ought to be allowed to spread into these newly won lands. The quarrel died down, and the issue was shelved for a while. But sooner or later it would have to be faced and decided.

The time of decision arrived very soon. In 1848 gold was discovered in California's Sacramento Valley. Swarms of people from all over the United States, and indeed from all over the world, rushed to the coast in a frantic search for easy wealth. By the end of 1849 California's free white population had skyrocketed from practically zero to eighty-five thousand. A state constitution was drawn up and adopted which shut slavery out and made it unlawful. In December 1849 the Californians were hammering at the Union's door. "Let us in," they were shouting, "and without slavery!"

But the slaveholders bitterly opposed this idea. Leading the opposition was John C. Calhoun, a U.S. senator from South Carolina and the most influential spokesman for the proslavery cause. On March 4, 1850, he made a speech in the U.S. Senate in which he warned that the South would regard California as a test case. Solemnly he warned the American people that the South would quit the Union if Congress barred the slaveholders from taking their slaves to California and using them to make money there. "If," he told the Senate, "you exert the power to ban slavery in California today, tomorrow, who knows, you will seek to ban it in South Carolina itself. We in the South will choose war and secession rather than submit to such interference with our basic and fundamental institutions."

By 1850, then, the issue of the slaveholders' rights in the new lands taken from Mexico could no longer be avoided. Congress must now decide whether California was to enter the Union as a free state or not. It was a crisis that brought North and South onto a collision course. The whole country held its breath as it waited to see whether or not there would be war.

In January 1850 Senator Henry Clay of Kentucky proposed a solution to the crisis that has been labeled "the compromise of 1850." What he outlined was a kind of peace treaty between the North and South which would satisfy both sides to some extent and keep them from coming to blows.

Texas, Clay pointed out, was in the Deep South; it seemed clear enough to him that Texas ought to be admitted to the Union as a slave state. Very well, he said; in return for this concession by the North, let the South agree to admit California as a free state. Surely this would be a fair deal.

Clay then proceeded to his next big point. For many years antislavery people had been arguing that the slave trade ought to be made illegal in Washington, D.C. Was it not a disgrace, they asked, that in a free country slaves should be bought and sold at auctions within sight of the Capitol? It was up to the federal government, they said, to show a good example by abolishing the slave trade where it had the power to do so—and that was in the District of Columbia itself.

Very well, said Henry Clay: let the slaveholders agree to the abolition of the slave trade in Washington, D.C. But in return for this concession, the North would also have to yield something. Here Clay proposed the passage of a new Fugitive Slave Act which would make it much easier than it had been for slaveholders to recapture slaves who ran away and took refuge in the North.

On her way to Brunswick, Harriet stopped off in Brooklyn, New York, to visit with her younger brother, Henry Ward Beecher. Henry Ward had graduated from Lane Seminary in 1837 and then spent ten years as a minister in Indiana. In 1847 he was called to the pastorate of the fashionable Plymouth Church in Brooklyn, and began at once to embark upon antislavery activities that captured the attention of the entire nation.

In September 1848, for example, Henry Ward came home to find a brokenhearted black man, Paul Edmondson, sitting on his steps and weeping. His daughters, Mary and Emily, were being held as slaves in Washington, D.C., and would be sent off for sale in the Deep South unless their father could find $2,250 to purchase their freedom. Henry Ward went out at once to address an antislavery meeting and raised the money that very same night.

After leaving Brooklyn Harriet stopped off in Boston to see her brother Edward who had also come back from the Midwest and was now pastor of the Salem Church. Both her brothers, she found, were furious over Clay's compromise, which was then being debated in Congress. They were particularly angry at the terms of the new Fugitive Slave Act, which gave the federal government direct responsibility for catching runaway slaves and returning them to their owners at the expense of the taxpayer.

With the discussion of Henry Clay's compromise and of the new Fugitive Slave Act still humming in her ears,

Harriet took the boat from Boston to Bath in Maine. She arrived at Brunswick late in May. Faculty wives greeted her warmly. They were both shocked and saddened by the frail and worn appearance of the great Lyman Beecher's daughter, and by the children's patched and shabby clothes. They told Harriet that the Titcomb House on Federal Street had been engaged for the use of the Stowe family; and they offered help and hospitality while the Stowes moved in.

Harriet inspected the beautiful old wooden house and was very pleased with it. "It is," she wrote Calvin, "in a very good state of repair, and considering that it is a chance hit, suits our purposes wonderfully." The rent on the house, it was true, was more than Harriet expected to pay. But, she assured Calvin, this did not really worry her very much. "I mean," she told him, "to raise a sum myself equivalent to the rent this year; it only imposes the labor of writing an extra piece or two."

This "extra piece or two" that Harriet would write in order to help pay the rent on the Titcomb House would blossom very soon into a magazine serial that would run for ten months and would be published in book form under the title of *Uncle Tom's Cabin.*

Early in June Harriet moved into the Titcomb House and busied herself with getting it into shape for the family and for the baby that she was then carrying. Calvin came east from Cincinnati early in July with Henry Ellis and Eliza. A week later the Stowes' seventh child, Charles Edward, was born. During the months of July and August, while Harriet was absorbed in caring for her new-born baby, Congress finally accepted Henry Clay's compromise and passed it into law. Texas was brought into the Union as a slave state, California as a free state. The slave trade was abolished in the District of Columbia. And in September 1850 the Fugitive Slave Act was passed.

This Fugitive Slave Act was one of the most important and most hated measures ever to be passed by a United States Congress. It raised the temperature of Northern people to fever heat. In some places people came out into the fields and the streets, guns in hand, to defy the law and to stop the federal government from seizing and returning runaways. Harriet Stowe's immediate purpose, when she began to write *Uncle Tom's Cabin*, was to speak out against this act, and to teach the American people that it was the symbol of a system of tyranny that threatened the survival of the American nation. Both this act and her writing about it speeded the conclusion among millions of Northerners that slavery was a mortal enemy that must be resisted to the death. It is indeed hard to understand the meaning of *Uncle Tom's Cabin* without a grasp of this law, which provided the immediate occasion for the writing of Harriet's novel.

When the Constitution was drawn up in 1787 it guaranteed to slaveholders the right to have returned to them runaways who fled their plantations and took refuge in the North. What this meant in practice was spelled out by the Fugitive Slave Act which Congress passed in 1793. Slaveholders, under this law, were authorized to "seize and arrest" runaways. They were then supposed to apply to a magistrate for a piece of paper authorizing them to take the fugitive back South from whatever state he had been arrested in. But most slaveholders did not bother with this formality. They just crossed the Ohio River or the Pennsylvania line, seized their runaways and dragged them home. For years fugitive black people were taken back to the land of slavery as casually as if they had been lost children or stray animals.

The first Fugitive Slave Act of 1793 made possible terrible abuses, and a profitable business grew up in kidnapping free black people who lived in the northern states and had never run away at all. Slave catchers simply seized these people, dragged them south under the pretense that they were "runaways," and sold them to slave traders.

This was a shame and a scandal, and antislavery people loudly denounced so wicked an abuse of the law. To cope with the situation, therefore, state after state in the North passed measures to protect the rights of free black people and to prevent them from being whisked off in the dead of night. These "liberty laws," as they were called, guaranteed *all* black people charged with being fugitives a court hearing, a jury trial, counsel for their defense, and the right to produce witnesses on their own behalf—all the rights, in fact, guaranteed to white people charged with having committed a crime.

By the 1830s then, it was becoming a serious offense in most northern states to seize a black person and to remove him or her from the state without first having gone through the procedure prescribed by state law. The Liberty Laws certainly protected free black people from kidnapping; but they also made it much harder for slaveholders to catch runaways. The fact is that as antislavery sentiment grew in the North white people who saw blacks being seized and dragged back to slavery got mad. They rescued runaways from jail and even threatened the slave catchers with violence. And, of course, even if there were no actions of this type, court procedure was in itself slow and time-consuming. It now made it much more expensive than before to retrieve a runaway.

In 1842 the slaveholders' dismay over this situation turned to glee. In January of that year the United States Supreme Court handed down a decision—*Prigg v. Pennsylvania*—that declared all the Liberty Laws to be unconstitutional. With a wave of the hand, as it were, the Court swept them all away. A slaveholder's right to seize a runaway, said the Court, was guaranteed in the Constitution. It was a *national* right, which the federal government had the duty to protect and to enforce. No state had the power to defeat or nullify this right by laws that placed obstacles in the way of its realization.

After this it should, theoretically, have been easier than before to catch runaways. But the Prigg decision had exactly the opposite effect. "The job of catching slaves and seeing that they are returned is a *federal* duty," said the states; "very well! Let the federal government do it all: we want no part of it." State after state now passed new Liberty Laws telling all their people—private citizens, jailers, police officers, and judges—not to cooperate in any way at all with slaveholders seeking to recapture runaways.

Thus by 1850 the northern states had moved into open defiance of the Fugitive Slave Act of 1793 and of any kind of slave-catching at all that might take place on northern soil. Such now was the feeling throughout the North concerning the immorality of permitting slaves to be hunted upon free soil that slave-catching in many states had come almost to a halt.

In September 1850, when Charles Edward Stowe was barely two months old, a second Fugitive Slave Act was passed by Congress as part of the Compromise of 1850. This law, which aroused antislavery leaders like Henry Ward and Edward Beecher to a new pitch of fury, spelled out the ways in which the federal government itself would be authorized to go into the business of catching runaways and returning them to their owners. It is easy to see why such a law would be welcome to the slave masters. It provided massive federal aid, in men and money, to anybody seeking the capture of fugitives. And, of course, the taxpayer footed the bill.

Under this new Fugitive Slave Law of 1850 special federal commissioners were appointed to hear cases involving runaways and to issue the proper papers to owners seeking to take black people back to the South. If hostile crowds threatened the slave catchers, the commissioners were empowered to "employ so many persons as they may deem necessary to overcome such force." In plain language, the government might call out the army, the navy, and the marines to protect slaveholders and to prevent the liberation of runaway slaves.

But this wasn't all. Suppose a runaway had hidden himself in a hayrick and his owner was loudly demanding that he be dragged out? Federal officials in such a situation were entitled to ask anybody standing by to help them. If you refused to help catch a fugitive when you were ordered to do so, it was a federal crime; you could be punished by fine or imprisonment in a federal jail. "This law," as Ralph Waldo Emerson put it, "makes slave catchers of us all."

Opposition to the Fugitive Slave Law of 1850 was instant, violent, and continuous. A series of acts of defiance electrified the nation. In 1850 a black man named Shadrach was tracked to Boston, arrested, and jailed; but before the federal commissioner could arrange to have him sent back South, a mob broke open the jail and set him free. In April 1851 Tom Sims, a fugitive from Georgia, was seized in Boston and sent back South; but it took an escort of three hundred armed men to "protect" Sims from the crowd that would otherwise have liberated him as he was marched through the streets and placed on board a steamer. And this was moderate compared with what was to come. When in 1854 Anthony Burns was arrested in Boston and sent back to Virginia on the order of the federal commissioner, it took an army of one thousand men to march Burns to the dock.

In the fall of 1850, when all Boston was seething over the case of Shadrach, Isabel Beecher, Edward's wife, wrote to Harriet and urged her to speak out against the Fugitive Slave Act. "If I could use a pen as you can," wrote Isabel, "I would write something that would make this whole nation feel what an accursed thing slavery is." Harriet wrote back promising that she would do what her sister-in-law asked. "As long as the baby sleeps with me nights," she wrote, "I can't do much of anything, but I will do it at last."

Where would she publish the sketch or sketches of slavery that she was now planning? Harriet's first step was to write to Dr. Gamaliel Bailey, whom she had known in Cincinnati as editor of *The Philanthropist.* Bailey was now editor of *The National Era*, an antislavery weekly newspaper published in Washington, D.C. She sent him a couple of short stories and asked if he would be interested in publishing them. Bailey's response was encouraging. He accepted the stories and sent a check for $100 in payment.

But still Harriet hesitated. She wanted, more than anything, to take up her pen and to write about slavery, but she was terrified at the thought of it. It was one thing, in those days, for women to write novels or short stories; to enter the field of politics and to write an attack upon slavery—that was something almost unheard of.

Early in January 1851 Henry Ward Beecher came to Boston to deliver a lecture; and then he took the train to Brunswick to visit his sister. Late in the evening, when the children were in bed and the snow lay thick outside, Harriet confided in her now-famous brother. She told him what she had in mind; was it right for a woman, she asked him, to write about slavery? Henry Ward's answer was both enthusiastic and emphatic. "Do it, Hattie!" he said.

Harriet's time to begin writing about slavery had now come. One Sunday in February 1851 she took the children to church. "My heart," as she told her son Charles Edward years later, "was bursting with anguish excited by the cruelty and injustice our nation was showing the slave, and praying to God to let me do a little and cause my cry to be heard." As she sat in the pew with her children around her, Harriet began to daydream. The church, the service, the children, all were forgotten. There came before her eyes, as real as life, the scene that Sarah Grimké had told about years before in Theodore Weld's *American Slavery As It Is*. It was a black man being brutally beaten and dying under the lash because he would not deny the existence of his true master, Jesus Christ.

That afternoon Harriet went to her room and wrote down what she had seen. In creating this episode, in turning it into a dramatic picture and putting it down on paper, Harriet had taken the crucial first step that is so familiar to creative writers. She had as yet not the faintest idea of the size and scope of the project that she was now embarking upon. But she had broken through a psychological barrier, a fear of her own inadequacy to handle the theme which she was tackling. She had made the all-important beginning in which, as literary artist, she saw also the possibility of carrying it through to the end.

Rapidly now the story that she planned to weave around Uncle Tom and his tragic death began to take shape. Early in March Harriet wrote to Dr. Bailey once again. Would he, she asked, be interested in publishing a story about slavery in serial form? "Up to this year," she told her old friend, "I have always felt that I had no particular call to meddle with this subject. . . . But I feel now that the time has come when even a woman or a child who can speak a word for freedom and humanity is bound to speak. . . . Such peril and shame as now hangs over this country is worse than Roman slavery, and I hope every woman who can write will not be silent."

Gamaliel Bailey wrote accepting Harriet's proposal, and

he also sent her a check for $300 as payment in advance for her story. No more than Harriet did Bailey at that time have the faintest conception of the undertaking to which he was committing himself. He certainly did not conceive Harriet's "story" as anything more than a series of sketches showing the evils of slavery in five or six installments.

Harriet was now fairly launched upon her writing, and there was no stopping. She performed the endless household chores, but she would not allow them to distract her from the central task. In one letter she talked of having been interrupted "at least a dozen times; once for the fish-man, to buy a codfish; once to see a man who had brought me some barrels of apples; . . . then to Mrs. Uphams to see about a drawing I promised to make for her; then to nurse the baby; then into the kitchen to make a chowder for dinner"; and always she returned to her desk. "Now I am at it again," she wrote, "for nothing but deadly deter-mination enables me ever to write; it is rowing against wind and tide."

As Harriet wrote, her theme took on its own independent life, followed its own logic, presented its own demands. The dam that for years had blocked the compassionate heart and the creative mind was broken. The deep feelings, the pent-up thoughts and dreams of seventeen years came roaring through the breach.

The first installment of "Uncle Tom's Cabin; or, Life Among the Lowly," appeared in *The National Era* on June 5, 1851. After that the story came out in weekly installments running almost without interruption until March 1852. Harriet did occasionally skip a week when she fell behind in the grueling and apparently unending job of writing for a weekly deadline. These delays brought anguished protests from her readers.

Before Harriet's work was one-third done she made arrangements with John P. Jewett of Boston to have her story published as a novel. *Uncle Tom's Cabin* was given to the world in book form on March 20, 1852. Jewett was rather frightened by the risk that he was taking in putting out so bulky a novel by so little known a woman author. But his fears soon vanished. The first printing of the *Cabin* was a mere five thousand copies, but these were grabbed up in two days. The public's appetite for the book seemed to be insatiable. By March 1853, one year after publication, three hundred thousand copies had been sold in the United States alone. By the time the Civil War broke out eight years later the figures for both American and British sales ran into the millions. *Uncle Tom's Cabin* was soon translated into forty foreign languages and was being read by people all over the world. Very few books in the history of modern literature have won such instant and such universal popularity.

Uncle Tom's Cabin made Harriet America's leading literary figure. Not since 1776 when Tom Paine published *Common Sense,* calling for independence from Great Britain, had a piece of writing made so deep an impression upon the public. In 1853 an abridged edition for children came out, entitled *A Peep into Uncle Tom's Cabin*, and that same year there were Welsh and German versions specially for immigrants. Tom songs became popular; and there was also a card game, Uncle Tom and Little Eva, in which the winning player was the one who first brought together a complete suit consisting of all the members of a slave family. A stage show produced by George Aiken played to packed audiences in Troy, New York, for one hundred nights, and traveling players were soon making their living from Tom shows all over the North. These, too, popularized the book and helped to boost its sales.

For the first time in their lives tens of thousands of Americans, regardless of age, race, creed, or sex, began to read a story that set forth vividly the human horror of slavery and exposed the inhumanity of those who profited by it. People reacted to the message with anger, shock, and tears. It was a moment of truth that would not occur again until February 1977 when Alex Haley's *Roots* flashed before millions on the nation's TV screens.

Harriet's creation was both bold and unique. No American writer before her had ever attempted a novel about slavery or anything that even remotely foreshadowed the *Cabin*. Of course, when the *Cabin* appeared there was already a great deal of antislavery literature in America; but most of this was in the form of antislavery tracts or pamphlets. These lectured the reader about the evils of slavery and gave the reasons why as a system of exploitation it defied the laws both of God and man. There were, too, a number of antislavery poems by people like John Greenleaf Whittier and Henry Wadsworth Longfellow which denounced slavery and those who defended it.

In addition to these antislavery poems and tracts there was a growing literature composed by fugitives and runaways themselves and published with the help of northern abolitionists and antislavery societies. The most famous of such memoirs, in which ex-slaves told of the horrors they had personally experienced and of their lives in bondage, was Frederick Douglass' *Narrative*. Josiah Henson's *Story of His Own Life* was another important work of the same type. Harriet had met Henson in Boston at Edward's house in 1850. A slave of saintly character, Henson had succeeded in fleeing from Maryland and finding his way to Canada. Harriet drew heavily upon his personality and his experience in order to create the character of Uncle Tom.

Writings like those of Douglass and Henson were often moving and informative accounts of the life and sufferings of an individual or a family, but they lacked the scale of Harriet's canvas and the sweeping vision of an entire social system which she set before the reader. The same was true of Richard Hildreth's *The Slave*, a fictionalized account of a slave's life written by a white historian and published in 1836.

Harriet's work was extraordinary not only because it was a new and pioneer type of novel but because it was written by a woman. Until 1852 few American women had broken the barriers of convention that forbade women to write about anything so real and so brutal as slavery. Angelina and Sarah Grimké had written about slavery and had agitated against it. Lydia Maria Child had edited an antislavery newspaper and had published her own antislavery tracts. But the most popular women writers wrote polite or conventional novels in which discussion of the topic of slavery was taboo. The most famous of such women novelists, in Harriet's time, was Catharine Maria Sedgwick, who wrote polite tales of upper-class life in New England.

For a woman to depart so boldly from custom took both

courage and conviction. It is part of Harriet's supreme achievement that she dared to give a bold and scorching expression to her feelings as a woman and a mother when she saw innocent and often defenseless human beings ground up or torn to pieces by the workings of slavery. "I wrote as I did," she said in 1853, "because as a woman, as a mother, I was oppressed and broken-hearted with the sorrow and injustice I saw, because as a Christian I felt the dishonor to Christianity, because as a lover of my country I trembled in the coming day of wrath. It is no merit in the sorrowful that they weep, or in the oppressed and smothering that they gasp and struggle, nor to me that I *must* speak for the oppressed—who cannot speak for themselves."

Harriet wrote both as moralist and propagandist, to arouse her apathetic countrymen, to awaken public sentiment to what she considered a horrible evil that threatened the liberties not only of black people but of all Americans. She knew, as she put it, that "all the capital, all the political power, and much of the ecclesiastical, is against the agitation of this subject." But she would not be silenced. The secret of her immense success was that she did not lecture, she did not condemn. She simply showed the operation of slavery through a series of pictures so vivid and compelling that even a child could understand them.

"My vocation," as she told Dr. Bailey, "is simply that of *painter,* and my object will be to hold up in the most lifelike and graphic manner possible Slavery. . . . There is no arguing with pictures, and everybody is impressed by them, whether they mean to be or not."

CHAPTER SEVEN

THE TRIAL
OF THE INNOCENT
Uncle Tom's Cabin, 1851–52

*If the scourge shall slay
suddenly, He will laugh at
the trial of the innocent.*

—*Job 9:23*

Uncle Tom's Cabin is cast in the form of a series of dramatic and lifelike scenes that pass before the reader's eyes in vivid succession. The curtain rises on a Kentucky plantation where the owner, Arthur Shelby, and a slave trader called Haley are engaged in some hard bargaining with each other. Shelby, a southern gentleman and a really decent person, is in debt to Haley; to pay the debt and to avoid ruin, he is forced to sell Haley one of his most valuable slaves, Uncle Tom. The slave trader insists upon his throwing in a little black boy, Harry, who is the son of a slave woman, Eliza, and her husband, George Harris.

Shelby breaks the news of this deal to his wife, Emily, who is very much upset and scolds her husband bitterly for his cruelty; not only has he torn the little boy from his mother and father, but he has broken faith with Uncle Tom, who has been promised his freedom. But it is no use. Shelby explains to his wife that he is in Haley's power. He must either do what Haley wants or lose the whole plantation.

Eliza is hiding in a closet and overhears the whole quarrel between husband and wife. Acting at once, she takes her child and flees northward through the frosty night toward the Ohio River. She is resting in a tavern by the water's edge when Haley, in hot pursuit, catches up with her. She escapes by taking Harry in her arms and crossing the river on the heaving, breaking ice, leaping from floe to floe.

Haley is cheated of his prey. He goes back to the village tavern and there meets up with Tom Loker and Marks, a couple of professional slave catchers. These two agree to go after Eliza and bring her back. "A revolting scene, don't you think?" Harriet asks her readers. But, she adds, maybe it isn't as disgusting as you think. "The catching business," she says, "is fast rising to the dignity of a lawful and patriotic profession. If all the broad land between the Mississippi and the Pacific becomes one great market for bodies and souls . . . the trader and catcher may yet be among our aristocracy."

Meanwhile, on the other side of the river kindly people take Eliza in and help her on her way. A farmer called Symmes, who has watched her leaping across the ice, helps her up the steep riverbank and directs her to a large white house where he thinks the people will help her. "You've earned your liberty," Symmes tells Eliza, "I don't see no kind of occasion for me to be hunter and catcher for other folks."

The white house to which Eliza has been directed is the home of Senator Bird of Ohio who has voted for a state law forbidding people to help runaways, but whose heart melts in the presence of Eliza and the agony of fear and sorrow which she is undergoing. The following exchange takes place between them:

"Were you a slave?" [Senator Bird asks.]
"Yes, sir; I belonged to a man in Kentucky."
"Was he unkind to you?"
"No, sir; he was a good master."

Bird is puzzled. If master and mistress were kind to her, and she had a good home, why did she run away? Eliza explains that her decision to flee, openly to defy slavery and its law, had nothing to do with the kindness of her master. She was defying, she explains, the ultimate cruelty of the law of slavery, which makes it legal to rend families apart and to tear a child from the parents who have given life to it and loved it.

Mrs. Bird, too, the senator's wife, is deeply moved by Eliza's plight—it is only a month or so since she lost a child of her own. "Then you will feel for me," Eliza says to her, "I have lost two, one after another—left 'em buried there when I came away; and I had only this one left."

Mrs. Bird decides not only to provide warm clothes for Eliza, but to give Harry the clothing of her own dead son.

She goes into the little bedroom adjoining her own, puts a key in the lock, and opens a drawer:

> Mrs. Bird slowly opened the drawer. There were little coats of many a form and pattern, piles of aprons, and rows of small stockings; and even a pair of little shoes, worn and rubbed at the toes, were peeping from the folds of a paper. There was a toy horse and wagon, a top, a ball. . . . She sat down by the drawer, and, leaning her head on her hands over it, wept till the tears fell through her fingers into the drawer; then suddenly raising her head, she began, with nervous haste, selecting the plainest and most substantial articles, and gathering them into a bundle.

Senator Bird drives the fugitives by night over the muddy back road to the farm of John Van Tromp, who is pictured as a slaveowner who had freed his slaves and fled from Kentucky because "he could not tolerate the workings of a system equally bad for oppressor and oppressed." Van Tromp, in turn, transports Eliza and Harry to the home of Quakers, Rachel and Simeon Halliday, and there she is reunited with her husband, George, who has also fled. Loker and Marks pursue them, and George fights off the slave catchers at gunpoint. The couple move on with their child and find safety in Canada where slavery is outlawed.

After this we hear no more of Eliza and her George till the end of the book, many chapters later. But with these few swift and vivid scenes Harriet has already scored heavily. She has drawn a true picture of the slave trade, of the cruelty and power of slave law, of the despair of black people and the bitterness of their defiance. The thrilling message, like the shot at Lexington, echoes around the world.

With Eliza, George, and Harry safe in Canada, Harriet turned in earnest to the story of Uncle Tom. At this point it is necessary to warn the reader that Harriet's Uncle Tom is not the person whom you think he is. Most of us have gotten our impressions of Uncle Tom not from the novel but from the "Tom shows" or dramatizations that were so familiar a part of the American scene from the time of the Civil War until the 1920s. The Tom shows portrayed Uncle Tom as a grinning, fawning, spineless yes-man. Actually, Uncle Tom as Harriet portrayed him is a person almost the opposite of the familiar stereotype. Harriet's Uncle Tom, to be sure, taught that black people should avoid violence and turn the other cheek to their oppressors; and he believed that slaves ought to show charity toward their owners and pray for their souls. Nevertheless, Uncle Tom as Harriet conceived him is a freedom fighter who will resist evil till his last breath, and will die before he raises his hand against his fellow people. He is a Christian martyr who, to a twentieth-century reader, brings Martin Luther King immediately to mind.

Uncle Tom is introduced to us as a strong, healthy man in the prime of life, who is living in his cabin on the Shelby plantation with his wife, Chloe, and their three children. Told of his master's decision to sell him, Tom accepts his fate without protest but with a heavy heart. He gives in without a struggle, not because he is an "Uncle Tom," but because he is ready to sacrifice himself in order to save the other slaves on the plantation from a similar fate.

In a little while Haley with his gang of shackled slaves is on board *La Belle Rivière*, a Mississippi steamboat, headed for New Orleans and the slave market. Harriet now introduces us to Augustine St. Clare, a New Orleans slaveowner returning home after a trip to Vermont. With him is his daughter Evangeline, known as Eva. St. Clare has been visiting his cousin Ophelia, and she is coming back with him to New Orleans to help run the household. Eva falls overboard, and Tom dives in and saves her. Eva begs her father to buy Tom and this is soon arranged.

The scene shifts to St. Clare's luxurious New Orleans mansion, in the enclosed courtyard of which "a fountain threw high its silvery water, falling in a never-ceasing spray into a marble basin, fringed with a deep border of fragrant violets." In this setting we meet Marie, St. Clare's wife. She is a selfish and self-centered woman who loves nobody but herself and leads a useless existence lying on her couch thinking that she is ill when she is not, and demanding endless attentions from those around her.

Marie St. Clare is a perfect contrast to cousin Ophelia, who believes that woman's life should be guided by the *ought*—by the need to do your duty to others no matter what the cost to yourself. But here, as elsewhere in her book, Harriet goes out of her way to show that Northerners are no more saintly than Southerners. As St. Clare himself puts it in a conversation with cousin Ophelia,

Northerners may be indignant at the wrongs that blacks suffer, yet "you loathe them as you would a snake or toad."

Harriet now launches upon a fundamental exploration of the meaning of slavery as an American institution. This is put into the form of a discussion between St. Clare and his cousin Ophelia.

Ophelia is furious because an old slave woman named Prue has been whipped to death by her owners. "Why on earth don't you do something about it?" she asks Augustine with anger; "ought not murder to be reported to the police?"

Augustine St. Clare shrugs his shoulders. In theory, he tells her, slaveowners are never brutal to their slaves, because brutality damages the slave, and nobody in his senses wants to damage valuable property. In actual practice, though, slaveholders do indeed abuse their power, and they do indeed commit cruel acts against their slaves. But, he goes on, there's no remedy for that. "If people choose to ruin their possessions," he says, "I don't know what's to be done. . . . [Slaveholders] have absolute control. . . . There would be no use in interfering; there is no law that amounts to anything practically, for such a case. The best we can do is to shut our eyes and ears, and let it alone."

Cousin Ophelia at once comes to the conclusion that St. Clare is defending slavery, but he hotly denies this. Yes, he says, politicians and clergymen and planters use all sorts of fancy words to justify slavery—they say that the slaves are happy, and that it's God's will, and so on. But, in the last resort, he goes on, *there is no possible defense for slavery.*

Slavery, he explains to Ophelia, is based upon power—the power of one class of men, who are strong, to seize and to oppress another class of men, who are weak:

> "Because," says St. Clare, "my brother Quashy is ignorant and weak, and I am intelligent and strong— because I know how and can do it—therefore, I may steal all he has, keep it, and give him only such and so much as suits my fancy. . . . Because I don't like work, Quashy shall work. Because the sun burns me, Quashy shall stay in the sun. Quashy shall earn the money and I shall spend it. Quashy shall lie down in every puddle that I may walk over dry-shod. Quashy shall do my will, and not his, all the days of his life. . . . I defy anybody on earth to read our slave code, as it stands in our law books, and make anything else of it. Talk of the abuses of slavery! Humbug! *the thing itself* is the essence of all abuse."

St. Clare, it seems, is a thoughtful and intelligent person who understands very well that the system he lives under is terribly and totally wrong. He lives under the system, he profits by it, but he sees it clearly for what it is. It is true, he says, that some slaves may get better food and more decent living quarters than free workers in European or American factories; but he brushes aside as absurd the idea that such slaves are therefore contented with their fate. "It's all nonsense," he says, "about slaves enjoying this! Tell me that any man living wants to work all his days, from day-dawn till dark, under the constant eyes of a master . . . on the same dreary monotonous toil, and all for two pairs of pantaloons and a pair of shoes a year, with enough food and shelter to keep him in working order!" No, he concludes: we planters simply use human beings for our own convenience.

It is time for Harriet to move on with her plot. The scene shifts to the family's summer villa on the shores of Lake Pontchartrain, "an East-Indian cottage, surrounded by light verandas of bamboo work, and opening on all sides into gardens and pleasure-grounds . . . where winding paths ran down to the very shores of the lake. . . ." Eva is dying of tuberculosis, and she knows that she is dying. She loves all her father's slaves, including Topsy, a mischievous little black girl whom St. Clare has given as a present to his cousin Ophelia. Eva wants them freed, and she wrings from her father a promise that he will take her wish seriously. She then proceeds to die in a long-drawn-out deathbed scene that overflows with morbid sentimentality and shows Harriet at her very worst.

St. Clare now decides that, like James G. Birney, he will free all his slaves and then find a way to participate in the antislavery struggle. But he, in turn, meets his death while trying to stop a barroom brawl, and in a second the fortune and the future of his slaves change. Marie decides not to free them, but to sell them off and then return to her father's plantation. The scene shifts to a slave auction. Tom is sold to a brutal owner, Simon Legree, a New Englander, and hauled off to Legree's Red River estate.

Legree buys Uncle Tom because he sees that the man is not only strong but intelligent; he has hopes of making him a driver of other slaves, even a manager of his plantation. Legree, as it were, takes Tom to the mountaintop and shows him the world that he shall have, if only he obeys.

Tom refuses. He will not take power from the hands of Legree, and he will not use power to flog other human beings and to force work out of them. A grim battle of wills follows. Legree is determined that Tom shall obey him, or die; Tom, determined to die but not to obey. Cassy, Legree's slave mistress, puts an ax in Tom's hands and urges him to kill Legree, but he refuses. He is totally nonviolent; he will die for his beliefs, but he will not kill. And in the end Legree and his drivers flog Tom to death.

Finally Harriet brings all the threads of her story together. George and Eliza go back to Africa and settle in Liberia; Topsy, raised by Ophelia in New England, follows them as a Christian missionary. Young George, the son of Arthur Shelby, takes over the plantation on his father's death and frees all the slaves.

Now, at the end of her book, Harriet emerges from her role as a writer about slavery and speaks directly to her audience. What, she asks, can ordinary people do, faced as they are with the horrors that she has described? "There is one thing that every individual can do," she points out; "they can see to it that *they feel right*." Americans must stop turning their backs on slavery, treating it with indifference, or even apologizing for it. They must learn to use their hearts, to feel pity and compassion for the victims of the system, and to think of the wrongs done to these people as wrongs done to themselves.

Receive the black strangers, she goes on, into our Christian churches, educate them. Then help them to return to Africa "where they may put into practice the lesson they have learned in America." Only so can the Union be saved, for the whole American people is involved in the crime of slavery, not just a portion of them. We must purge ourselves, she says, of this injustice, or there will be a day of reckoning and a day of vengeance. The judgment of God will be upon us.

To understand the nature of Harriet's achievement it is helpful to compare *Uncle Tom's Cabin* with the Fourth of July address that Garrison had delivered twenty-three years before in Edward Beecher's Boston church.

Garrison warned the American people, in that speech, that slavery had become a mortal threat to the American union; that either slavery must go, or the American people and their Republic would face destruction. Harriet's message in the *Cabin* was the same. "You must," she told the people, "feel in your hearts the horror and evil of slavery, and you must abolish it; if not, you will face a day of reckoning compared with which a thousand cholera epidemics will be as nothing."

There were a number of important differences in the reception of Harriet's message and Garrison's. Garrison, and the abolitionists who followed him, spoke to limited audiences; their books and pamphlets and newspapers reached, relatively speaking, only a handful of people. The abolitionists, too, often paid a heavy price for daring to discuss in public a topic that powerful and wealthy leaders had decided was taboo. Theodore Weld was driven from Lane, and James G. Birney from Kentucky; Garrison himself nearly lost his life at the hands of a lynch mob in Boston in 1836; Elijah Lovejoy was killed at Alton, Illinois, the following year.

Harriet, too, might have been afraid of rock-throwing or threats upon her life or demands that she be thrown in jail. What is striking about her book is its magnificent audacity. She took hold of a forbidden subject and explored it boldly. She wrote an antislavery tract that, for the first time in the history of the country, reached the homes and touched the hearts not of a few, but of millions. She made antislavery thinking the common property of every family in the land.

In the *Cabin* Harriet handed down a blunt but deeply considered Christian judgment upon slavery and all its works. This, of course, was in itself not new: since colonial times people had been attacking slavery as a social evil that mocked the laws of God and the rights of man. Harriet, indeed, like so many of the writers who went before her, was a Christian moralist. But the *form* of her attack was so different from theirs as to be revolutionary; she was the first person to write a truly effective novel about slavery, rather than just a sermon, or an exposé, or a tract.

This novelistic form was vital to the success of Harriet's work. She painted a series of scenes into which she introduced real and highly articulate people—they laugh, groan, fight, mock, lament, and talk to each other. These scenes are so vividly constructed that Harriet carries us in imagination from one end of the Union to the other. By this means she shows us slavery in its everyday operation. We see how the system takes living, breathing people, how it grinds them up body and soul, and destroys them. She shows how the law of slavery violates Christian law with respect to the *human* use of human beings: do unto others as you would that they should do unto you. This law, she reminds us, is the very bedrock of our American faith.

Harriet's message, that slavery is wrong and must be abolished, came at a critical moment in the history of the United States. Public opinion, spurred by the war with Mexico and the Fugitive Slave Act of 1850, was beginning to awaken to the fact that the abolitionists were right, that the slave masters of the South and the slave empire that they ruled had taken the place of the British Empire as the major enemy of the American people, of their democratic institutions and of their free-labor economy. Harriet's book was a response to this new mood, but it was also an independent contribution to the antislavery cause of the first magnitude. The *Cabin* not only reflected the American mood, but it speeded up that lightning change or revolution in public opinion, which slaveholders had foreseen and which they so much feared.

There was yet another important difference between *Uncle Tom's Cabin* and Garrison's 1829 address. Garrison had proclaimed the new and radical doctrine that black people were American citizens, that they had as much right as any white person to be in the United States and to own and inherit the American soil upon which they had labored so long and so painfully without pay. This was a message that Harriet Stowe never fully absorbed. She remained for many years a colonizationist; one, that is, who believed that black people had no right to stay in America, that they ought to be returned to Africa.

From Harriet's day till our own a number of black leaders like Martin Delaney and Marcus Garvey have taken the same position. They have contended that black people ought to return to Africa because winning true equality in the United States is impossible and even to dream of this is a delusion. But white colonizationists, on the whole, have been racists; they have contended that America ought to be reserved for the Anglo-Saxon race, and that there is no place in it for "lesser breeds" like Africans. In the *Cabin* Harriet sometimes refers to black people in the condescending tones of white superiority. There is some nonsensical talk about African "docility of heart," childlike simplicity of affection, and so on. We in the twentieth century find this both unacceptable and offensive.

In being a colonizationist Harriet was not at all unusual—both Thomas Jefferson and Abraham Lincoln held identical views. Colonizationists never denied that slavery was wrong; they only insisted that the future of blacks as free people lay not in the United States but under an African sky. The racism behind this notion of the future of black Americans is a fault in Harriet's book; but it does not diminish at all the central and revolutionary thrust of the *Cabin*. The *Cabin* was a call to all Americans to place themselves in harmony with their own Declaration of Independence, and to face the fact that the holding of human beings in bondage is wrong. The *Cabin* was a trumpet blast announcing the day of judgment and the end of the world—the world of slavery. In writing this book Harriet saw herself as a messenger of God bearing tidings both of doom and joy. She announced, and she demanded, a revolution in American public opinion.

CHAPTER EIGHT

THE FIREWINGED FEET
The *Key to Uncle Tom's Cabin*, 1852–53

And where I see the firewinged feet
They only hear the wind.

                    —*James Elroy Flecker*

Uncle Tom's Cabin was a success from the very day that it first came out. Within a month the publisher, Jewett, had sold twenty-five thousand copies and was falling behind in filling the orders that came pouring in. He had three power presses running twenty-four hours a day, six days a week, to keep up with the demand. As for Harriet, she made no less than $30,000 in royalties from sales in the year 1852 alone.

Soon a chorus of praise made itself heard. Letters began to arrive at the Titcomb House from many parts of the country as people told her how much they liked the book and how much it had moved them. Harriet hired her sister

Isabella as a secretary so that all these letters might be opened and read and answered.

Harriet had become famous overnight, and naturally enough she was overjoyed with her success. The long years of scrimping and saving were over; poverty with its humiliations and frustrations would no longer haunt the Stowes. Now, at last, Harriet could buy what luxuries she pleased, could furnish her home as she wished, and could travel. Wherever she went people greeted her with deep respect and went out of their way to do her favors. While Calvin went on living his studious life among his books, Harriet moved out into the world with a new poise and a new confidence born of her achievement.

Edward Beecher, Harriet's older brother, worried about all this acclaim. In June 1852 he wrote to his sister from Boston and warned her against the sin of pride and of the danger of having her head turned by success. In truth, there was little reason for Edward's concern. It became clear soon enough that there were plenty of people who hated Harriet because she had written the *Cabin* and who were eager to attack her reputation and cut her down to size. She would have to spend much time and energy in defending herself. In this new struggle now forced upon her there would be little opportunity for smugness or self-congratulation.

Proslavery people both in the North and the South were quick to grasp the fact that the *Cabin* was the most dangerous assault upon the institution of American slavery that had ever appeared. The inevitable counterattack began to develop in the summer of 1852 as conservatives both at home and abroad awoke to the power and fatal direction of the book's thrust. By that time letters were arriving in the mail that showered Harriet with insult, abuse, and obscenity; some of them even went so far as to threaten her life. The full force of open public attack came in the fall when the defenders of slavery began to denounce her with savage intensity in pamphlets, speeches, and book reviews. As Harriet read these attacks, the first joy of success gave way to amazement, anger, bewilderment, and pain.

Some critics accused Mrs. Stowe of being a rabble-rouser and a revolutionary. It didn't matter, they said, whether her book was true or false; it ought to be suppressed because it was subversive of law and order and established authority. The *Cabin,* these critics charged, would stir up hatred of the southern slave masters and rulers in the hearts of people both black and white; it would produce disturbance and strife; it would set race against race and section against section. "Mrs. Stowe," as the London *Times* put it, "knows that an impassioned song may set the world ablaze."

Other critics agreed that the *Cabin* was subversive, and they added that it was also totally untrue. *The Literary Messenger,* a Southern magazine, accused Harriet of being a deliberate liar. *Uncle Tom*, thundered the *Messenger*, "is a fiction throughout; a fiction in form, a fiction in its facts, . . . a fiction in its morals. . . . Fiction is its form and falsehood is its end."

Some writers asserted that Harriet had written the *Cabin* for no better reason than to make money and to satisfy her personal greed. Typical of such accusations was the piece that appeared in the *Southern Quarterly Review* in January 1853. The reviewer wished her joy of the huge royalties that she had earned. "This," he said, "was, we presume, in the lady's opinion, worth risking scolding for."

This charge was one that hurt Harriet deeply, because there was more than a grain of truth in what the *Southern Quarterly Review* said. One reason why she had begun the writing of the *Cabin* was to make a little money, to fulfill the promise that she had made to Calvin to pay the rent on the Titcomb House. In doing this she had combined self-interest with the call of duty. But her critics had taken this truth and given it an evil twist. That she had stirred up hatred, slandered the South, and invented a pack of lies out of a passion for money and personal profit—this was a formidable charge to have to meet.

One aspect of Harriet's work that received special attention from her critics was her treatment of slavery law. The *Cabin* had presented this law as something inconceivably cruel. Slavery law exposed millions of black people to sufferings and wrongs from which no individual master, however kind, could adequately protect them. It conferred upon white people the right to own black slaves, to punish them at will, to buy and sell them for cash, to give or bequeath them to their children, to chase them with dogs when they fled, to track them to hiding places even in free territory, and to drag them back to a life of unpaid labor. Harriet's onslaught upon the law of slavery was the heart and essence of her message. This law, she showed, defied the law of God, the teachings of Jesus Christ, and the ethics of democracy.

Inevitably, proslavery writers rose to the defense. The law of slavery, they said, was really no worse than the law of any other civilized community, nor did it inflict any greater wrong upon human beings. *The Literary Messenger,* for example, readily agreed that under slavery children were torn from their parents, husbands separated from their wives, and fathers snatched away from their families. But, said the *Messenger,* the operation of law is the same in its effects all over the world—wherever people commit crimes, it asked, are they not punished by imprisonment or hard labor for what they have done, and are not families in consequence split apart? This happens, said the *Messenger,* not only in the South, but also "in the deserts of the Sahara as amid the snows of Greenland, in the streets of Lowell or Boston, as in those of London, Manchester and Paris."

There was an obvious weakness in this position. In most civilized countries men and women are sentenced to imprisonment only after they have been convicted of a crime in open court, and have received a trial according to the procedures established by law. Black slaves, by contrast, were delivered body and soul into the hands of their masters in a fashion without parallel in other societies. All their lives these slaves were obliged to suffer physical punishment, were compelled to do hard work, and were deprived of their freedom without having committed any crime at all. Was this not, in itself, an extraordinary abuse of power?

The answer the proslavery people gave to this question has been called "paternalism."

The slaveholder, these people argued, was in reality the

father of one big and usually happy family; he felt toward his slaves the same feelings as a father normally holds for his children. From this viewpoint the slaveowner's main obligation was to provide protection for his slaves throughout their lives. Slavery, said the defenders of the system, far from increasing the sufferings of the slaves, actually had the opposite effect. White masters were the slaves' most devoted friends, concerned "to protect them against want as well as against material and mental suffering; to prevent the separation of families, and to shield them from the frauds and crimes of others. . . ."

Of course, these defenders of slavery agreed, a situation did arise once in a while when acts of cruelty, even mutilation and murder, were committed by white people under the influence of sudden anger. But such acts, as in other countries, were punishable by law. The slave, the *Southern Quarterly Review* pointed out, enjoyed not only the protection of a kindly master, but also of the law itself. Harriet had argued that when men like Simon Legree beat slaves like Uncle Tom to death there was no law and no public opinion to hold such murderers accountable for their acts. Not so, said the *Review:* "our laws protect, as far as legislation can, the very beast from cruelty and barbarous treatment. How much more do they protect the slave!"

The proslavery attacks upon Harriet could be summarized in one sentence: she was an inspired liar who had painted a picture of the South that was false as a whole and false in its details, and she had done this both to make money and to inflict harm out of sheer malice.

These accusations cut Harriet to the heart. It was true that she had used her wonderful imagination to see slavery as a whole, to grasp the full meaning and agony of the black experience. But nothing could have been further from the truth than the idea that she had invented the picture she had painted, or that she had merely imagined what she had written. Her vision was based upon painstaking study both of people who had had experience of slavery and of their writings in books, pamphlets, and newspapers.

For example, in July 1851, when installments of the *Cabin* had already begun to appear in *The National Era*, Harriet wrote a letter to Frederick Douglass. Addressing the famous ex-slave and black leader as her "brother," she asked for his help. "In the course of my story," she told him,

> the scene will fall upon a cotton plantation. I am very desirous, therefore, to gain information from one who has been an actual laborer on one, and it occurred to me that in the circle of your acquaintance there might be one who would be able to communicate to me some such information as I desire. I have before me an able paper written by a Southern planter, in which the details and *modus operandi* are given from his point of sight. I am anxious to have something more from another standpoint. I wish to be able to make a picture that shall be graphic and true to nature in its details.

While we do not know if Douglass responded to Harriet's request, the letter is important as a vivid instance of the care that Harriet took with her novel and of the effort that she made to base her story upon the truth of human experience. But how was she to tell the world that this was so—that she was a *student* of slavery, not a mere fiction writer?

For most of the year 1852 Harriet had little time to worry about the hostile reviews of her book that were appearing. After the family had been in Brunswick for two years Calvin resigned from his position at Bowdoin College and went to Andover Theological Seminary in Massachusetts as Professor of Sacred Literature. So, in the summer and fall of 1852, Harriet was busy moving from Brunswick and settling into her new Andover home. She secured an old stone house on the edge of the campus and happily busied herself remodeling it. Only in October when all the family had made the move did she begin to give serious attention to the mounting attacks upon the *Cabin* and how best to meet them.

Harriet's first idea was to prepare a short essay in answer to her critics which could simply be tacked on to future editions of the *Cabin,* or which could even be circulated separately as a pamphlet if the need arose. This essay would prove that Harriet had modeled her characters after people who had really lived, and that she had built her plot around events that had actually happened. "I am writing a supplement to *Uncle Tom,*" she told her friend Eliza Follen in November 1852, "in which I set forth all the documents on which the scenes and different characters are founded." Such a supplement or addition to the *Cabin* would be like a batch of footnotes. It would provide the authority upon which some of the main incidents and experiences in the novel had been based.

Very soon Harriet abandoned this plan; and by the end of the year she was working upon something much more ambitious. "I am writing a work now," she wrote to Eliza in December, "which will contain perhaps an equal amount of matter with *Uncle Tom's Cabin.*" She had, in other words, decided to write not just an essay, but a second book on slavery.

This change of plans was a decision of great importance in the history of American literature and the study of the American South. It led to the production of a work on the law of slavery that was brought to completion in over five months of ceaseless labor from the first beginnings in October 1852 till the following March, 1853, when Harriet's final draft lay on her publisher's desk. It was entitled *A Key to Uncle Tom's Cabin: Presenting the Original Facts and Documents Upon Which the Story is Founded Together With Corroborative Statements Verifying the Truth of the Work.*

Why did Harriet make so sweeping a change in her original plan—one, too, that saddled her with so huge a burden of extra work?

The question of "fact or fiction" in the *Cabin* was not quite as simple a matter as Harriet thought it was before she sat down to write the *Key.* On one level we may ask: Is the novel accurate in its facts—did people like Uncle Tom actually exist, or could they have existed? Did families get split up by sale? Did mothers driven to despair by the loss of their children actually drown themselves? Did men like Simon Legree flog people like Uncle Tom without breaking the law or having to be afraid of punishment for their crimes?

For Harriet to answer questions such as these was not too difficult. All she had to do was to provide satisfactory information about her sources. Part I of the *Key* did exactly this. Here she took twelve of the most important out of the seventy characters that she had created in the *Cabin,* told how she had come to create them, and who the real-life people were who had served as models. She cited abundant sources that included her own experience with black families during the Cincinnati years, Theodore Weld's *American Slavery As It Is,* the narratives of black fugitives, such as Frederick Douglass' and Josiah Henson's, and the testimony of travelers, including letters from Louisiana that her own brother Charles had written to the family in 1838.

Having provided the sources from which she had created her principal characters Harriet wisely gave over. She could have applied the same treatment to the *Cabin*'s entire cast of seventy characters, but it would have been a fruitless exercise. To prove that the novel had been in fact written from start to finish from observation of real people and real life would have been interesting but, beyond a certain point, irrelevant. The characters in the novel, after all, were only the building blocks in a wider plan; she used them only for the purpose of putting together a message, of painting a picture of slavery as a whole. This was the main reason for her book. The *Cabin,* after all, might be true in a lot of its detail and still be false in the total picture that it conveyed.

On this level, therefore, the issue at stake was the truth of the total thesis about slavery that Harriet had presented. Her critics' main attack was directed at this rather than on the specific incidents and characters that sustained it. The *Cabin,* said they, might conceivably be true in some or all of its details, and yet be false and subversive in the main message it conveyed.

Thus Harriet was forced by the logic of her own position as well as by the nature of the attack upon it to move forward to new ground, and to defend not only the truth of the *facts* she presented but also the truth of the *case* she had made in using those facts. What, above all, she had to defend was the truth of her indictment of slavery as a social system.

In the main part of the *Key,* therefore—that is, in Parts II and III—Harriet moved forward to her central task. In the *Cabin* she had painted slavery as essentially a relentless struggle between the slave masters on the one side and their victims on the other: a struggle on the one side to rule, to control, and to exploit, and, on the other, not to be ruled, controlled, and exploited. What was this vision of slavery based upon? Where had she gotten it?

In answering this question Harriet focused upon the law of slavery, upon the legal codes which, state by state, sustained the whole system and bestowed upon white people the power to own, to buy and sell, to punish and to exploit black people. But in expounding this law she did not plan, at the end of 1852, to confine herself to the materials she had had at her disposal when the *Cabin* was written. She intended, as any good scholar should, to buttress her thesis about the social and legal system of slavery with new materials that had come into her possession during the year 1852. These materials had been sent to her by many friends, including a number of leading American lawyers. They comprised, as Harriet told her friend Eliza Follen, "an immense body of facts, reprints of trials, legal decisions and testimony of people now living South, which will more than confirm every statement made in the *Cabin*. . . ."

The system of law that prevailed in the South, Harriet explained in the *Key,* had nothing at all to do with justice. Its central purpose was to enable one class of people, slaveholders, to control another class of people, black slaves. The purpose of law in slave society was not to protect the slave from exploitation or abuse, as the paternalists had argued: on the contrary, the main function of the law of slavery was to protect the slaveholder himself from the seething, boiling vengeance of his victims.

The mightiest element in nature, she went on, is the soul of man. This human soul, when confined by any form of tyranny, including slavery, becomes "a fearfully explosive element," a force of volcanic power that threatens at any moment to erupt. Harriet, with poetic vision, presented the black people to her readers as "a seething, boiling tide, never wholly repressed, which rolls its volcanic stream underneath the whole framework of slavery society, ready to find vent at the least rent or fissure."

The slave codes, she argued, were deliberately fashioned for the purpose of holding down, containing, and repressing this "seething, boiling tide." The law unleashed a violence that was inflicted upon slaves every day of their lives. The ultimate savagery of these laws, Harriet emphasized, was no accident but the fixed expression of a deliberate purpose. The uncontrolled power that the law placed in the hands of the masters enabled them to wield a weapon of terror and with this to hold the entire black population in subjection. The excessive harshness of the laws flowed from the assumption that it was both necessary and right for white slave masters to abuse black people and to crush them if they dared to resist.

The sources for Harriet's analysis were the South's own lawbooks and the records of cases that had been tried in Southern courts. She used these sources to shatter the view that slave society was humane and paternalistic, that the welfare of the slave "family" was its main purpose; and she quoted effectively from Southern authorities themselves to prove her point. A distinguished Southern judge, Edmund Ruffin, for example, pointed out that there was no likeness at all between the power of a parent and the power of a slave master:

> In the one case the end in view is the happiness of the youth, born to equal rights with that of the governor, on whom the duty devolves of training the youth to usefulness in a station he is afterwards to assume among free men . . . with slavery it is otherwise. *The end is the profit of the master, his security and the public safety* [emphasis added].

A Key to Uncle Tom's Cabin was published in the summer of 1853 when Harriet and Calvin were touring England. It was a bulky volume containing more than 250 pages with a double column of type on each page. The book sold ninety thousand copies within a month of its publication, and for a few years it enjoyed a wide circulation both in England and the United States, but its success was in no way as great as the *Cabin*'s. By the end of the Civil War in 1865 the book was out of print, and only a few more years passed before it was entirely forgotten. When *The Collected Works of Harriet Beecher Stowe* were published in 1896 the *Key* was not included, and not even mentioned.

Harriet along with everybody else did her best to forget about her book. As she examined all the new evidence that she had accumulated during 1852—statutes, court decisions, reports of trials—she was filled with horror. "It is worse," she wrote to one Eglish friend, "than I supposed or dreamed." And to another she added, "I write it in the anguish of my soul, with tears and prayers, with sleepless nights and weary days." To Charles Kingsley, a famous British writer, she complained in the spring of 1853 that she had been for months "literally dead and buried under the weight of that awful book I have been forced to write because people insisted on having fact instead of fiction." Years later, when somebody asked her when the *Key* was written, Harriet could not even remember the date. "I am sorry," she said, "I have no positive means of information."

From Harriet's own time until the present day, scholars have paid little or no attention to the *Key*. Most of them have dismissed it as a work not deserving of serious attention. Katharine Anthony, for example, who wrote an article on Mrs. Stowe for the *Dictionary of American Biogra-*

phy, called the *Key* "a complete failure." John R. Adams, an authority on Harriet's literary career, made the charge in 1963 that she wrote the *Key* simply to bolster her own ego which had been badly damaged by critical reviews of the *Cabin.*

Another authority who attacked the *Key* was Gilbert Hobbs Barnes, a well-known historian of the antislavery movement. He denied that Harriet had written the *Key* at all. In his view the book in its entirety was cribbed from Theodore Weld's *American Slavery As It Is.* "A Key to Uncle Tom's Cabin," wrote Barnes in 1933, "is composed largely of excerpts from Weld's pamphlet."

Neither Adams' nor Anthony's opinion about the *Key* need, perhaps, be taken too seriously. They had merely leafed the pages of Harriet's bulky work without realizing the intellectual or historical dimensions of what she had accomplished. In this they are to be criticized no more than many other scholars who could not find time to study Harriet's book and to digest its meaning. But Barnes' accusation needs to be looked at more carefully. Is it indeed true, as he charged, that the *Key* is a plagiarized version of *American Slavery As It Is?*

The answer to this question recoils upon Barnes himself. It shows that this particular scholar made his accusation against Harriet when he was familiar neither with Weld's work nor with hers. A careful comparison of the two books shows that Harriet's citations from *American Slavery As It Is* occupy a maximum of five of her double-column pages.

Today *A Key to Uncle Tom's Cabin* is back in print and once more accessible to students who are examining it with

CHAPTER NINE

THEY ARISE LIKE GRASS
Literary Career, 1856–78

In the morning they arise like grass which groweth up. In the morning it florisheth and groweth up, in the evening it is cut down and withereth.

—Psalm 90

While Harriet was working on the *Key* at the end of 1852 she received an invitation from the Glasgow Antislavery Society to visit Scotland with all expenses paid. The thought of going to Europe filled her with excitement. Harriet had never traveled beyond the United States: to visit Great Britain, the birthplace of her childhood heroes Sir Walter Scott and Lord Byron—here was a fine adventure to look forward to! Work on the *Key* was hard and painful, but anticipation of a European trip made it all much easier to bear. She discussed plans with Calvin. It was decided that they would first go to Scotland and that they would follow this visit with a tour of both England fresh interest. The suggestion has been made that the *Key*, so far from being a failure, is a contribution of great importance for the understanding of the history and the law of American slavery. In the words of an eminent lawyer, Arthur Kinoy, Harriet shows in the *Key* "a rare ability to lay bare the essence of a system of law characteristic of the most advanced students of jurisprudence."

To create the *Key* with its profound analysis and fresh probing of slavery, Harriet drew upon sources of unbelievable extent and variety. These included correspondence, personal interviews, newspaper items, autobiographies, pamphlets, legal, theological, and historical treatises, to say nothing of dozens of trial records and court decisions. The system and clarity with which she organized these materials is all the more remarkable when it is remembered that she was not a professional scholar like Theodore Weld or Calvin Stowe, and that she had absolutely no academic training beyond the high school level. Yet she produced a legal treatise that may stand the test of time as a pioneering, contribution to the history of American slavery and the struggle of black people against it.

and the Continent. The children would be left behind in the care of friends and relatives.

Harriet also took her brother Charles Beecher, now pastor of the First Congregational Church in Newark, New Jersey, along with her as her secretary. The party left Boston at the end of March, reaching Liverpool after an ocean crossing on the steamer *Niagara* that lasted twelve days. When they arrived huge crowds were waiting at the docks to see Harriet and, if possible, to shake her hand.

Wherever she went in the British Isles, both in the country districts and in the industrial towns, the story was the same. Thousands of people gathered to welcome her, to demonstrate their affection, to speak with her, and to invite her to visit their home communities. In her letters home Harriet told of "invitations of all descriptions to go everywhere, and to see everything, and to stay in so many places."

Many people who had no chance either to see Harriet or to shake her hand wrote to her. When she reached Glasgow there was a pile of letters stacked so high that it took Charles, as she said, "from nine in the morning til two in the afternoon to read and answer them in the shortest manner; letters from all classes of people, high and low, rich and poor. . . ."

While she was in Britain, and particularly in London, Harriet met and enjoyed the hospitality of all kinds of fashionable and well-known people—dukes and duchesses, statesmen, famous writers, archbishops, and so on. But the welcome that she received was primarily an outpouring of the warmth and the affection of the common people, and of this Harriet herself was keenly aware. "What pleased me most," she wrote about this welcome, "was that it was not mainly from the literary, nor the rich, nor the great, but the plain common people. . . . The butcher came out of his stall and the baker from his shop, the miller dusty with flour, the blooming comely young mother with her baby in her arms, all smiling and bowing."

This fine reception that the British people gave to Harriet was far more than just a personal tribute. It was also a demonstration of support for United States democracy and for the American antislavery cause. At that time people in England, as in many other countries, had a deep admiration for the United States. Many of these people, who were both poor and oppressed, saw in America the land of their dreams. With the Revolution of 1776 a new Republic had arisen across the seas; it symbolized abundant land, self-rule, freedom from tyranny. Men and women there did not have to bow and scrape before any lord, and they did not have to fight in wars not of their own choosing nor submit to cruel taxation to finance those wars.

But if the United States was the home of a remarkable experiment in democracy, it was, at the same time, a land where slavery flourished. British people understood this very well. The British Empire itself had been founded upon slavery. English traders had coined money out of the blood of African slaves ever since they had won almost complete control of the international slave trade in the eighteenth century. British sugar capitalists had made fortunes out of the toil of African slaves on the great plantations of the West Indies. And as for the British cotton goods that were being sold all over the world when Harriet arrived in England in 1853—were these goods not made out of cotton which black Americans had groaned and sweated and died to produce?

The credit of making the shame of slavery known to the British people goes to the British antislavery movement, which between 1800 and 1837 launched an all-out campaign for the abolition of the slave trade and of slavery in the British Empire. This antislavery message resounded throughout the British Isles. Though of course not everybody was converted, by 1850 the British people knew only too well about the horrors of slavery and the endless wrongs that it had inflicted upon innocent African people.

Thanks to this antislavery movement the international slave trade received a fatal blow and was, by 1850, a dying institution. Slavery, too, had been abolished in the British West Indies. But of course none of this touched the problem in the United States. Slavery was growing in the United States at the very same time that it was being abolished in the British Empire. This fact, as the British people well understood, presented a crisis not only for the United States but for the entire world.

At this critical time Harriet Beecher Stowe arrived on British shores. She was an American woman who had boldly explored and condemned the greatest evil in her country, and who had called for its abolition. This was exciting news for the British people, and they grasped at once the meaning of her work. They saw that the overthrow of the tyranny of American slave masters would be an event of world significance. Would not the collapse of slavery in America, they asked themselves, weaken the stranglehold of tyrants over the common people everywhere?

In asking this question the British people, of course, were not thinking only of others, such as Arabs who endured the cruel rule of the Turks, or the dozens of Russian peoples ground under the heel of the Tsar; they were thinking also of themselves.

When Harriet Stowe arrived in England in 1853, not a single British worker enjoyed the right to vote; voting was a "privilege" that the middle and upper classes reserved exclusively for themselves, and they had no desire to confer the privilege upon anybody else. Most British working people toiled for long hours in mines and sweatshops and factories under terrible conditions, and they had no trade unions to help them fight for a better life. Men, women, and children worked their lives away for little pay, lived in hovels, and were bitterly poor—so poor, in fact, that American slaveholders boasted that they would never stoop so low as to treat their slaves the way British workers and Irish peasants were treated.

These British working people saw clearly that the overthrow of slavery in the United States would spell the triumph of democracy in that country. This, in turn, they felt, would advance the cause of democracy and worker organization in Britain itself. This, then, was one important reason for the enthusiasm with which they greeted Harriet.

By the end of May 1853 Harriet brought her British tour to an end. It was time to quit London, where she had spent almost a month, and to leave for the Continent. At this point Calvin said good-bye to his wife, packed his bags, and headed for home. He had, it must be confessed, become really rather bored with the whole trip. There was this endless applause and praise for Harriet, which he resented and felt was "spoiling" her as a dutiful and loyal wife. And there were these endless speeches which English notables delivered at every meeting, dinner, or public occasion at which the Stowes were present. Calvin found these speeches offensive. Too often the speakers lectured the United States for its wickedness in continuing to tolerate slavery; too often British audiences rewarded such speakers with wild applause in what Calvin regarded as anti-American demonstrations.

On all these occasions, no matter what the speakers said, it was Calvin who had to stand up and make a tactful reply on behalf of his wife. In those days women were not supposed to take part in public life, and they certainly were not supposed to speak in public—public speaking and public life were things which the males preferred to keep for themselves. A few brave souls, of course, defied these rules. But as far as "polite" society was concerned, woman's place was in the home—producing and rearing children, supervising servants, and playing hostess at dinners and garden parties.

So Harriet wasn't able to answer the speeches given in her honor. Calvin had to do it for her. This was something that he did not like at all, because it reduced him to being nothing more than a mouthpiece for his wife. "Mrs. Stowe has asked me to convey to you her deep appreciation . . . ," "My wife has asked me to tell you what an honor it has been . . . ," and so on and so forth.

On one occasion Calvin let his irritation at this state of

affairs get the better of him. It was a meeting of the British Antislavery Society where the denunciation of American wickedness had been blunter than usual, and more prolonged. Calvin was so angry that he forgot about having to speak for his wife and jumped up and spoke for himself. Britain, he told his listeners, was just as much responsible for American slavery as Americans were—most of America's cotton, after all, was bought by the British, worked up in British factories, and sold to British customers. All Calvin got for his pains was a sharp rebuke in the press for speaking out of turn.

By the end of May, therefore, Calvin was tired of being welcomed merely as the husband of a famous woman. "I would rather," as he wrote, "be at Andover about my business than anywhere else in the world; and I am tired to death of the life I lead here." The Continent, as he knew, would merely bring more of the same routine; there would be more of these endless songs of praise which Harriet seemed to thrive on. But the thought of it, as he said, made him feel "inexpressibly blue." And so he made his decision. "I shall not go to Paris," he told Harriet, "I shall return to Andover, and I wish I was there now!" So Calvin packed his bags, kissed his wife, and headed for home, leaving Charles Beecher to do the speechmaking in his place. Soon he was happy again in the seclusion of his Andover library, reading his books and getting his lectures ready for the fall.

We do not know how Harriet reacted to this situation with her husband, or what the feelings were that she hid beneath the friendly and smiling face that she showed to her public. But surely her thoughts were bitter. She, as a woman, had done what no man had done. She had stripped the mask from U.S. slavery and had exposed it not only as an evil but as a mortal danger to the human race. Nonetheless, she was still reckoned as a second-class citizen; the most elementary rights granted to males were denied to her and millions of her sisters simply on account of their sex. She, one of the nineteenth century's most articulate writers, was forbidden by convention to utter a single word in a public forum.

Harriet's experience was typical of the indignity that antislavery women suffered at the hands of men who regarded them not as equals but as inferiors. Such women often had to pay a heavy price for their commitment to the antislavery cause. Women like Sarah and Angelina Grimké, Abigail Kelley Foster, Sallie Holley, Caroline Putnam, Lucy Stone, and Sojourner Truth traveled around the country lecturing about slavery. They ran a gauntlet of scorn and abuse, mostly from males, and not infrequently were in physical danger. As for the great antislavery writer Lydia Maria Child, when she presented a copy of one of her books to the Boston Athenaeum, her borrowing privileges were promptly canceled!

Harriet returned from Europe in September 1853. This trip marked a turning point in her life. She had won recognition for her talents beyond anything that she had ever dreamed possible. The menace of American slavery still tormented her, but she had done her duty and she had spoken out. She was at peace with herself, with the world, and with God.

The very completeness of Harriet's public success speeded up the process by which she again became a purely private person.

By 1856, in the first place, Harriet had said all that she wished to say about slavery, and there would be little more to add. In that year she published her second and last anti-slavery novel, *Dred, A Tale of the Great Dismal Swamp.* It was based upon the life of Nat Turner, the black hero who in 1831 led a slave revolt in Virginia's Southampton County for which he paid with his life. The book contained many fine insights and much excellent writing. It was a great success and sold more than 100,000 copies within a month.

Mrs. Stowe's Dred was a slave runaway who with his wife and children lived in North Carolina's Great Dismal Swamp until he was tracked down by whites and killed. In this book Harriet sounded an Old Testament theme. People who are trodden down by others have a right both to revolt and to revenge. She dealt, too, with the double suffering and the double wrong inflicted upon slave women who must both labor in the fields like men and also bear children year after year to be torn from them and sold like cattle in the open market.

Personal tragedy, in the second place, now began to operate to produce in Harriet a deep weariness with public affairs. The spring and summer of 1856 saw the Stowes on a second European tour; this time the twins, Eliza and Harriet, went with their parents, and also Henry Ellis. Henry Ellis was Harriet and Calvin's oldest son. He was a beautiful young man, eighteen years of age. In the fall of the year he left his parents and returned to the United States to enter Dartmouth College as a freshman.

Harriet, Calvin, and the twins stayed on in Europe until the spring of 1857, and then came back to Andover. They had hardly returned when news came from Dartmouth College that Henry Ellis had been drowned while swimming across the Connecticut River, which flows broad and swift and deep on the western side of the New Hampshire school. This blow almost deprived Harriet of her reason. "If ever," she wrote at the time, "I was conscious of an attack of the Devil trying to separate me from the love of Christ, it was for some days after the terrible news came."

From that time on Harriet's life was deeply shadowed. The pit of suffering that lies beneath the bright surface of existence she now probed to its very depths. Women, she told herself, are tragic beings because of their supreme capacity for love. Every child that a mother bears and loves is a hostage that she gives to fortune. She spoke for womankind when she wrote "suffering is inwoven in our very existence. It is the texture of our heart strings—there are such terrible possibilities with every affection, that one pities the living and still more the loving."

It was 1857 and the country was moving toward its great mid-century crisis. How, when she was coping with the ultimate pain of bereavement, did Harriet look? "She is not a beautiful woman," wrote one who visited her at this time, "and yet her eyes are not often surpassed in beauty. They are dark and dreamy, and look as if some sorrowful scene ever haunted the brain."

Even two years after Henry Ellis' death Harriet was still

trying to convince her heart of what her mind understood, that "I must never, never, in this life, see that face, lean on that arm, hear that voice." Days went by when she lived in hopeless, blank despair, when she could do nothing, not even water the plants that grew around the house, but let them die by inches before her eyes. What did it matter, she asked herself, now that Henry Ellis was gone, whether she watered them or not? "I am cold, weary, dead," she wrote to Georgiana; "everything is a burden to me."

Grief encouraged Harriet to seek her own private ways to forget. She turned back to the bright sunlit scenes of her youth, to the New England world that she knew and loved so well. She turned from writing about slavery to writing once more about New England.

The first of Harriet's New England novels was *The Minister's Wooing,* which she published two years after Henry Ellis' death, in 1859. The story is a simple one about a minister who falls in love with a young woman whose sweetheart is away at sea. Upon this bare framework Harriet wove an embroidery that told of the New England countryside, of New England homes, and of the customs of the New England community.

The Minister's Wooing was followed by *The Pearl of Orr's Island* in 1862. Harriet laid the scene of her story on an island off the coast of Maine, which she had visited and explored many times when she and Calvin were living at Brunswick. She told of the life, the love, and the death of Mara Lincoln, an orphan girl. Mara, like Harriet's own mother, Roxana, died of consumption; and, like Harriet's own son Henry Ellis, she died at the height of youth with the future that she had so passionately looked for unfulfilled. Mara, just as Harriet herself was trying to do, faced death without bitterness and without challenging the inscrutable will and wisdom of her God.

After the Civil War was over other New England books came from Harriet's pen. There was *Sam Lawson's Oldtown Fireside Stories* in which she brought together and retold some of Calvin's endless fund of tales which, over the years, had fascinated her so much. And then there were *Poganuc People* and *Oldtown Folks,* novels into which Harriet wove much vivid detail about New England and its people as she remembered them from her childhood days.

Harriet's New England books deserve to be read and reread. They are peopled with characters who live in her pages with their own intense vitality. She deals not only with the folk but also with the folkways of New England—the quality of people's religious belief, the clothes they wore, the houses they inhabited, the food they cooked and ate. And, because she loved New England very much, Harriet filled her books with exquisite word pictures of the New England seashore and countryside.

This explosion of Harriet's creativity as a novelist of New England coincided with the United States' mid-century crisis and the coming of the Civil War. In 1860 Abraham Lincoln was elected President as the Republican Party candidate, exclusively by northern votes. The Republican program was a simple one: slave masters, it said, must not be permitted to take slaves into new territories. They must not be allowed to start fresh slave societies on the American continent where no such societies had existed before. All new lands, said the Republican program, brought to the Union either by purchase or conquest must be reserved for settlement by free men and women and for the development of a social system based upon free not slave labor.

Slaveowners had for some years foreseen and dreaded the possibility that the federal government might one day place a ban upon the further growth of the slavery empire. They knew that this would surely happen whenever enough people woke up to the evils of slavery and began to demand that the government do something about it.

This popular awakening to the dangers of slavery began to develop rapidly during the 1840s, and it was, of course, something that Harriet herself contributed to in no small way. The Republican demand for "no further expansion of the power of slavery" was due in a real measure to the work of propaganda and of education that she had undertaken.

Southern spokesmen made no secret of how they viewed the Republican program. They warned Northerners that the election of Lincoln would be the signal for Southern secession from the Union. The consequence of this, they said, would be war as the two societies—the free enterprise society of the North and the slave society of the South—slugged it out to see which of them would control the land, the wealth, and the people of the continent.

As Lincoln traveled from place to place in 1860 during his political campaign, he made statements denying that the Republican program was the threat that slaveowners imagined it to be. "We do not," he said, "intend to disturb or challenge slavery where it now exists; all we intend to do is to put an end to its future growth."

Southerners paid little attention to such statements because they did not believe them. What would stop Congress, they asked, tomorrow or the next day, from banning slavery in the South itself if the northern majority demanded it? Antislavery people like Garrison had already made very clear that they believed the holding of black slaves was a direct violation of the American Constitution, and that the force of the Constitution ought to be invoked to guarantee the right to liberty for all Americans regardless of the color of their skin.

Thus when Abraham Lincoln was elected President in 1860 the Southern states started to secede and to form their own Confederacy for the purpose of raising money, organizing troops, and fighting the war that was to come.

The first two years of the war produced much confusion in the North on the subject of war aims. Lincoln, a very cautious and moderate man, had made it clear, even before the war began, that he was not "against" slavery; and he repeated many times his belief that he had no right to interfere with slavery as it existed in the South. What, Northerners then asked themselves, were they fighting for? Without writing "emancipation" on its banners, the North had no war aim, no moral cause, no special reason to fight.

This confusion menaced the very survival of the Union. The American Republic had powerful enemies in England. These people, merchants and industrialists, feared the competition of the young giant across the sea; they dreamed of smashing the Union, and they sought, accordingly, to swing England into the war on the side of the South. "You see?" they said to the millions of English people who had antislavery convictions, "this is not a war to end slavery but just a quarrel between the two governments into which the U.S. is now divided. We ought to recognize the Confederacy and use the British Navy to enforce our right to carry on trade with the South."

Both in 1861 and 1862 Harriet raised her voice in the cause of emancipation. Freeing the slaves, she said, was a matter of life or death for the Union—either the Union would attract black people to its side, and thus win the war, or the South would find ways to use these people. "We may rest assured," she wrote, "that if we delay till we alienate the Blacks, the enemy will find means to turn them against us effectively. . . ."

Finally Lincoln himself realized that British intervention on the side of the South was imminent, and that this, in all probability, would mean the defeat of the Union cause. To stop this from happening and to give the Union a war aim behind which the British people might rally, he decided upon the emancipation of the slaves. Lincoln's first or preliminary emancipation proclamation was issued on September 22, 1863. The slaves, he said, would become free on January 1, 1863, if the South had not laid down its arms by that time.

This was important news for Harriet. Some ten years before, when she was at work on *A Key to Uncle Tom's Cabin,* she had been sent, as a representative of American women, a petition from England. This petition, signed by hundreds of thousands of British women, urged their American sisters to take action to end the curse of slavery. It was entitled *An Affectionate and Christian Address of Many Thousands of Women of Great Britain and Ireland to Their Sisters of the United States.* Now, finally, Harriet was in a position to answer them.

But first she had to make sure that Abraham Lincoln was really in earnest, that he did intend indeed to issue his Emancipation Proclamation. So in November 1862 Harriet took the train to Washington to see the President. She planned to publish her *Reply* to the "Affectionate Address" in the *Atlantic Monthly*; on the way to Washington she wrote a letter to its editor, J. T. Fields, from Henry Ward's home in Brooklyn. "I am going to satisfy myself," she wrote, "that I may refer to the Emancipation Proclamation as a reality and a substance not to fizzle out at the little end of the hour, as I should be sorry to call the attention of my sisters in Europe to any such impotent conclusion." What she wanted from the President, she told Fields, was a definite assurance "that our war is to be put right through and that the Proclamation is to go with vigor."

A few days later the interview between Harriet and Lincoln took place. She received from the President his assurance that the Emancipation Proclamation would be issued on January 1st, and that the war would at last become a struggle for the abolition of slavery. On leaving the White House, Harriet at once went back to her hotel and put the finishing touches to her *Reply* to the "Affectionate and

Christian Address," which was given to the public within a month in the November issue of the *Atlantic Monthly*.

The *Reply* was simply and clearly written; we may think of it as a brilliant contribution to the Union cause. In her essay Harriet sketched the reasons why the Civil War had come about, and she described slavery as its root cause. By 1862 the abolition of slavery had become the Union's central military purpose. Black people, slave and free, were rallying to the Stars and Stripes, American women were sacrificing everything for this struggle, and were giving up their husbands and brothers and sons. We are doing our part to end slavery, she assured her British audience; but, she asked her British sisters, "Sisters, what have you done, and what do you intend to do?" She ended by making the same appeal to them that Garrison had made in the Boston meetinghouse in 1829. "We appeal to you as sisters, as wives, and as mothers, to raise your voices to your fellow-citizens, and your prayers to God for the removal of this affliction and disgrace from the Christian world."

On January 1, 1863, Lincoln freed the slaves. It was a historic moment. English public opinion would now swing rapidly to the North's support, and the Northern cause would itself win new strength as more and more black people flocked to its banners. The news came to Harriet while she was attending a celebration at the Boston Music Hall. She received a standing ovation from the crowd, it was the crowning moment of her life. Henceforth she could devote herself with a quiet mind exclusively to her own family affairs and literary interests.

In 1863 the Stowes bought a home in Hartford, Connecticut, and went into retirement. Harriet busied herself with remodeling the house and planting a garden. "I am busy with drains," she wrote a friend, "sewers, sinks, digging, trenching—and above all with manure!"

The Stowes' twin daughters, Harriet and Eliza, moved into the Hartford house with their mother and father. They never married, but devoted most of their lives to taking care of their famous parents in their old age. In 1865 Harriet's third daughter, Georgiana May, was married to the Reverend Henry Allen, a young Hartford minister, in her parents' home. Harriet was delighted. "The day was cool and bright," she wrote, "the bride lovely . . . in short all was well."

Four years after Georgiana May's wedding Harriet and Calvin lost a third son. Frederick William, born in 1840, was two years younger than Henry Ellis, who was drowned at Dartmouth College. Enlisting in the army when the war broke out, Frederick William was severely wounded in the head at Gettysburg. He lived on in a state of mental confusion, wandering from place to place, drinking and never settling down. In 1867 Harriet invested some of her funds to buy an orange grove at Mandarin in Florida on the St. Johns River. She had hopes that the southern climate and open-air work would help with the recovery of her son. But again he wandered off, went out to the West Coast, and vanished in San Francisco. The family never saw him again and they never learned his fate. In her inmost heart Harriet felt that God had punished her cruelly. Had He not taken from her all the sons born during the Cincinnati years before she decided to take pen in hand to speak out against slavery?

Thus Mandarin became Harriet's own home. Every year

she and Calvin spent three or four months there, or more. They would go by railroad to Savannah, Georgia, and then embark on one of the little steamboats that went "winding through the curious network of islands and lagoons that line the shores," traveling south until they reached the St. Johns River and were deposited at the Mandarin wharf. From 1867 to 1878 no less than fourteen books came from Harriet's pen, and much of this writing was done at Mandarin. She slipped quietly into old age amid the vivid colors and luxuriant foliage of the southern spring. "It is glorious budding and blossoming spring," she wrote in March 1872, "and we have days when merely to breathe, and be, is to be blest. . . . Life itself is a pleasure when the sun shines warm and the lizards dart from all the shingles of the roof and the birds sing in so many notes and tones that the yard reverberates. I sit and dream and am happy and never want to go back north. . . ."

Beyond the live oaks with their long gray mosses and the orange trees with dusky leaves and golden globes the St. Johns River meandered with a sluggish, scarcely perceptible motion to the sea.

Calvin Stowe died in 1886; Harriet survived him for ten years. The twins took care of their mother and nursed her devotedly till the end. During these last years Harriet's memory grew dim and her mind wandered; but she enjoyed the company of her youngest son, Charles Edward, who was the minister of a Hartford church. Both she and Calvin were buried in the cemetery at Andover where Henry Ellis lay.

Bibliography

John R. Adams, *Harriet Beecher Stowe* (New York: Twayne Publishers, Inc., 1963). A useful guide to Harriet's writings and literary career.

Charles Ball, *Fifty Years in Chains*. First issued in 1836 under the title *Narrative of the Life and Adventures of Charles Ball*. Reissued by Dover Press, with an introduction by Philip S. Foner (New York, 1970). One of the best-known contemporary accounts, by a Maryland slave, of the sufferings of a slave's life and of his desperate struggle to win freedom.

Edward Beecher, *Narrative of Riots at Alton* (1838). Reissued as a paperback, edited by Robert Merideth (New York: Dutton, 1965). In this classic antislavery pamphlet Harriet's brother tells the story of the martyrdom of Elijah Lovejoy and also expounds his own beliefs about slavery and the necessity for its destruction.

Henry Bibb, *Narrative of the Life and Adventures of Henry Bibb* (1850). Reissued by Negro Universities Press (New York, 1969). Ranks with Ball's memoirs as an outstanding account of the slavery experience and the bitterness of a fugitive's struggle.

Levi Coffin, *Reminiscences of Levi Coffin, Reputed President of the Underground Railroad* (1876). Reissued by Augustus M. Kelley (New York, 1968). A detailed and fascinating account of the struggles of fugitive slaves and the people who helped them. Indispensable for an understanding of Harriet Beecher Stowe's Cincinnati experience.

Barbara M. Cross, editor, *The Autobiography of Lyman Beecher* (1864). Reissued by the Belknap Press of Harvard University Press (Cambridge, Mass., 1961). A collection of writings by and about Lyman Beecher that is indispensable for the study of the Beecher family.

Merton Dillon, *Elijah Lovejoy, Abolitionist Editor* (Urbana, Ill.: University of Illinois Press, 1961). The only biography yet written of the antislavery martyr.

Frederick Douglass, *Narrative of the Life of Frederick Douglass, An American Slave* (1845). Reissued by the Belknap Press of Harvard University Press, Benjamin Quarles, ed., (Cambridge, Mass., 1960). A classic account of the experience of slavery by a fugitive who became famous.

J. C. Furnas, *Goodbye to Uncle Tom* (London, England: Secker and Warburg, 1956). Criticizes the racist aspects of *Uncle Tom's Cabin* and provides a useful picture of the "Tom shows." Furnas' overall evaluation of Harriet Stowe and her work is directly opposed to the position taken in this biography.

Josiah Henson, *Truth Stranger than Fiction: the Story of his Own Life* (1849). Reissued by Corner House Publishers (Williamstown, Mass., 1973). A classic account of slavery and flight by a saintly individual who influenced Harriet Stowe in the creation of Uncle Tom.

Constance Rourke, *Trumpets of Jubilee* (1927). Reissued as a paperback (New York: Harcourt and Brace, 1963). Interesting essays on Lyman, Henry Ward, and Harriet Beecher.

John Anthony Scott, *Hard Trials on My Way: Slavery and the Struggle Against It: 1800–60* (New York: Alfred A. Knopf, Inc., 1974). Elaborates the story of slavery and the antislavery movement during the lifetime of Harriet Beecher Stowe, and provides a bibliographical guide.

Wilbur H. Siebert, *The Underground Railroad from Slavery to Freedom* (1898). Reissued by Peter Smith (Gloucester, Mass., 1968). Recent attacks upon this work have not shaken its position as a great study of black fugitives and the people who helped them.

Harriet Beecher Stowe, *Uncle Tom's Cabin or, Life Among the Lowly* (1852). There is a fine modern edition issued by the Belknap Press of Harvard University Press, edited by Kenneth S. Lynn (Cambridge, Mass., 1962). Various paperback editions are also available, notably from Harper and Row (Perennial Classic) and Washington Square Press.

A Key to Uncle Tom's Cabin: Presenting the Original Facts and Documents upon which the Story is Founded (1853). Reissued by Arno Press (New York, 1970).

Dred, A Tale of the Great Dismal Swamp (1856). Reissued by AMS Press, Inc. (New York, 1970, 2 vols.).

The Pearl of Orr's Island (1862). Reissued by the Gregg Press (Ridgewood, N.J., 1967).

Sam Lawson's Oldtown Fireside Stories (1872). Reissued by the Gregg Press (Ridgewood, N.J., 1967).

Oldtown Folks (1869). Reissued by the Belknap Press of Harvard University Press, Henry F. May, ed., (Cambridge, Mass., 1966).

Benjamin P. Thomas, *Theodore Weld, Crusader for Freedom* (Rutgers, N.J.: Rutgers University Press, 1950). Provides valuable information for a study of the context of Harriet Stowe's antislavery writing.

Theodore Weld, *Slavery As It Is* (1839). Reissued by F. E. Peacock Publishers as a paperback (slightly abridged), Richard O. Curry and Joanna Dunlap Cowden, eds. (Itasca, Ill., 1972). The reissue of an edition of Weld's pioneer study is an important contribution and a help to students who seek to understand both the *Cabin* and the *Key*.

Winifred W. Wise, *Harriet Beecher Stowe: Woman With a Cause* (New York: G. P. Putnam's Sons, 1965). A short and readable study of the first fifty years of Harriet Stowe's life.

Index

About the Author

John Anthony Scott, an outstanding educator who now teaches at the Rutgers University School of Law and the Fieldston School in New York City, was born in England and educated at St. Paul's School and Trinity College, Oxford. He received his doctorate in history and policital science from Columbia University and has served on the faculties of the Ethical Culture School, Columbia, and Amherst College. He is the author of *Fanny Kemble's America* and general editor of a distinguished series of documentary histories for young readers, and the author of more than forty books and scholarly articles in the areas of history, musicology, and education. His community activities have included the organization and operation of draft-counseling services, and seminars on the use of folk song in the classroom.

Married and the father of three children, he now lives in New York City, and somehow finds time for sports—tennis, swimming, and backpacking—and for music, especially the classical guitar.